Contents

Preface

"Did Christian Churches and Churches of Christ really begin as a unity movement? Why didn't I know that?"

"You mean we used to be called Disciples of Christ? I thought that was just another denomination."

"Christian Churches and Churches of Christ believe and practice the same things we have from the beginning, don't we?"

Statements like these by members of congregations related to the Stone-Campbell Movement reflect a serious lack of knowledge of our movement's past and an increasing desire by many to know more of their heritage. This desire has led us to believe that there is a need for a brief account of the history of Christian Churches and Churches of Christ. This book hopes to serve newcomers as well as long-time members of our churches by giving them insights into our heritage. It is also an introduction to this significant group of churches for those unfamiliar with its place in American Christianity.

Any attempt, however, to look at one's spiritual ancestry is as pleasurable and painful as examining one's family tree. Some ancestors and family stories make us swell with pride; others we would just as soon forget. We are insiders to Churches of Christ, and to Christian Churches and Churches of Christ, and we write with a deep appreciation for those who have gone before us. We would in no way bash the churches of our mothers and fathers. But as honest historians, we must present our story as we see it, "warts and all."

Thus, as we look forward to God's blessings on Christian Churches and Churches of Christ in the future, we also look back to how he has led us kindly in the past. We do not consider the story of our past as merely interesting trivia—that's not what this book is about. Instead, we hope our work here will help provide a usable past for us in Christian Churches and Churches of Christ. There are marvelous aspects to our tradition that we need to recover today as we continually reform and conform the church according to the image of Christ.

This has been in many ways a joint project. As we worked on this book together, we have learned the difficulties and the joys of Christian unity. We have not always agreed, but we have been willing to discuss—a necessary attitude for those concerned about Christian unity. This willingness to discuss, to listen, and to learn from each other was modeled for us by the early leaders studied in this book.

We also had much help along the way. Several read the manuscripts and made valuable suggestions. We especially thank Deb Holloway, John York, John Mark Hicks, Lynn McMillon, Richard Hughes, Tom Olbricht, Mike Matheny, Henry Webb, and Robert Hull for their time and insights.

The authors and publisher gratefully acknowledge the work of Rob Sorensen, Jeff King, and Mac Ice, archivist at the Disciples of Christ Historical Society, in collecting and scanning the illustrations. We especially thank Erma Jean Loveland, special collections librarian for the Center for Restoration Studies at Abilene Christian University, for her expert assistance and constant spirit of helpfulness.

Since the first edition of this series, the premier reference work on Stone-Campbell history has been published: *The Encyclopedia of the Stone-Campbell Movement*, edited by Paul Blowers, Douglas Foster, and Newell Williams (Eerdmans, 2005). The articles are engaging as well as informative, and reading appropriate articles in the *Encyclopedia* alongside your reading in this book will enhance your enjoyment and grasp of the material.

W. Dennis Helsabeck, Jr.
Gary Holloway
Douglas A. Foster

Do We Have a History?

He came into a course in Restoration History and announced, "I don't care what Barton Stone or Alexander Campbell said. All I care about is what the Bible says."

We thought of several appropriate responses. What we did say was, "At least one reason you care only for what the Bible says is that Barton Stone and Alexander Campbell influenced you."

Or take another example. An undergraduate Bible major goes home to visit. At church on Sunday, a good deacon asks him, "What are you studying this semester?" The student replies, "The Gospel of Luke, Youth Ministry, Speech Communication, English Composition, and Restoration History." "Restoration History?" the deacon replies. "What good will that do you?"

These stories illustrate the mixed feelings in Christian Churches and Churches of Christ about our history. Indeed, some would deny that we have a history. Aren't we the church of the first century? Isn't all church history after the first century just a record of apostasy and corruption? Shouldn't we leap over those years to the purity of the early church? Don't we undercut our plea to be biblical by admitting we have a history?

Many Birthdays

We understand those who want to deny our history. On the side of the church building where one of us grew up were the words: "Church of Christ, Established A.D. 33." The idea was that we wanted to be the church of the New Testament, the one established

at Pentecost. That ideal still burns brightly in our hearts. We do not want to restore everything about the early church (no one wants to be exactly like the Corinthians), but we do want to be the kind of church that the first century churches should have been. In a real sense, we can trace our existence to that first church at Pentecost.

But do we have a history after Pentecost? Honesty requires that we answer, "Yes." The whole history of the church, as messy and fallen as it has been, is in some sense our history. Although we want to be like the early church, we must admit that we are not the first Christians. Two thousand years have passed. Previous generations have passed the faith on to us. We would not have the Bible itself were it not for the faithful labors of copyists and translators who lived long after Pentecost. One reason for studying church history is to honor these spiritual fathers and mothers.

Studying church history also helps us experience how faithful Christians in the past struggled to follow God in their own context. If we can see how the church in the past often conformed too much to its culture, then perhaps we can see how our own culture threatens to subvert the current church. Studying church history also shows how the church has positively affected the culture around it.

Studying history can also help us understand the Bible. We prize the authority of the Bible because those who went before us taught us to respect it. By seeing how previous generations understood (and misunderstood) the Bible, we gain a perspective on its meaning for our time.

This book focuses on our history in the context of America. While it is true in one sense that Pentecost A.D. 33 (or more likely, A.D. 30) is our birthday, there are other dates we can point to as beginning points of the existence of Christian

Churches and Churches of Christ in America. The first "founding document" of our history is *The Last Will and Testament of the Springfield Presbytery* written in 1804. The ministers who wrote those words began the first group of independent churches in this movement. Although many before him called Christians back to the Bible for the sake of Christian unity, Thomas Campbell's publication of *The Declaration and Address* in 1809 marked a significant intellectual beginning to our movement. The Disciples of Christ in particular see that date as their starting point (see chapter four), celebrating a centennial in 1909 and anticipating a bicentennial in 2009.

At the end of the nineteenth century, the movement divided with the Disciples of Christ (Christian Church) and Churches of Christ becoming separate groups. Some place that division in 1889, when Daniel Sommer and others called for a break of fellowship in the "Address and Declaration" at Sand Creek, Illinois. The "official" date of that division is 1906 (see chapters eight and nine). Then in the early twentieth-century the Movement divided again, producing the Christian Churches and Churches of Christ.

So what is our birthday? All and none of the above. We do want to be the church founded at the first Pentecost after the resurrection of Jesus. Yet, we must admit that we are the church in an American context. We owe our identity to Thomas Campbell, Alexander Campbell, and Barton Stone in the nineteenth century. We also owe a debt to those in the twentieth century who shaped what we now are as Christian Churches and Churches of Christ.

Tradition and Traditionalism

The student and the deacon mentioned above reflect our long-standing opposition to tradition. Why should we study our history if we in Christian Churches and Churches of Christ have always been against tradition? Shouldn't we be like that student who rejected Stone and Campbell to go to the Bible alone? The answer to these questions lies in the distinction between "tradition" and "traditionalism." Historian Jaroslav Pelikan has defined tradition as "the living faith of the dead," and traditionalism as "the dead faith of the living."

The Bible is both positive and negative about tradition (the biblical word means simply "something passed down"). When tradition becomes traditionalism, that is, when it takes the place of the original intent of God, then it deserves condemnation. Both Jesus (Matthew 15:1-6) and Paul (Colossians 2:8) condemn human traditions that supersede the will of God. On the other hand, Paul many times urges the churches to "hold on to the traditions" he had taught them (1 Corinthians 11:2; 2 Thessalonians 2:15; 3:6). These were not mere human traditions, but were the word and will of God.

So why study the history of Christian Churches and Churches of Christ? To honor our spiritual ancestors who passed the tradition of the faith on to us. Yet, those traditions must always be subject to the authority of Scripture. Indeed, one of our strongest traditions is the ultimate authority of the Bible over tradition. Nevertheless, responsible traditions are necessary to give shape to our church life and to help in passing on the faith. Indeed, church traditions are inevitable. The alternative would be starting the church over anew each day, resulting in chaos. Those traditions become harmful only when they change into fixed traditionalism that leads us away from the clear intent of Scripture.

In other words, denying we have a history leads to danger. Failure to recognize that our history shapes us results in our being prisoners to it. By being blind to the historical forces that shape our church practices, we fall prey to the danger of mistaking our circumstances and conclusions with the eternal will of God. By denying we have a history, we easily become traditionalists like the Pharisees who equated their teachings with God's Word.

The authors of this brief history are proud to belong to this movement. If we deny the good our spiritual ancestors accomplished, we become ungrateful children. If we ignore their mistakes, we become traditionalists who prize our own human history above the will of God. Only by taking an honest look at who we have been can we understand who we are. God has given us the ability to think historically and to grow in our understanding through this powerful gift. Using this gift of historical sense wisely is part of being faithful to God in our time and place.

The Early and Medieval Church

Acts chapter two portrays the first church in Jerusalem as a model church. They listened to the apostles, prayed, shared their food and money, grew numerically and had harmony with those around them (Acts 2:42-47). The rest of Acts and the New Testament, however, make it clear that the first century church had its problems. Individual congregations like Corinth faced divisions. The Judaizers claimed another way of salvation (Galatians 1:6-9). Others claimed a special knowledge unavailable to most (Colossians 2:16-23). Some even claimed to be Christians while denying that Jesus had come in the flesh (2 John 7). Even in the best of churches, there were those who did not get along (Philippians 4:2).

Thus, from the beginning church history has been messy. On the one hand, the church is a divine institution, the blood-bought bride of Christ. On the other, it consists of redeemed people who are still human, flawed, fallen, and sometimes even apostate. Although Jesus prayed that believers would have unity (John 17:20-23), from the very beginning of the church that unity has been a struggle.

During the first century of the church, the apostles were there to give guidance and direction. Their teaching and writings gave shape and unity to the churches. This is why it is right for us in Christian Churches and Churches of Christ to hold up the first century church as a model. They were not a perfect church, but they were apostolic. We want to be the ideal church we see modeled in the life of the apostles and other faithful New Testament Christians. We want to follow the apostolic teachings of the New Testament.

By the second century, however, the apostles were gone. The books of the New Testament existed, but the church had not yet collected and recognized them as Scripture (that process happened slowly over the next two centuries). One force that continued to give the church cohesion was the persecution of Christians by the Roman Empire. Although the persecution was sporadic and usually local, it did help keep the church pure. One did not become a Christian to get ahead in society. Instead, the examples of noble martyrs gave courage and boldness to the church.

That all changed at the beginning of the fourth century. A new emperor, Constantine (274-337), won his crown in battle after appealing to the Christian God. Although he tried to please both pagans and Christians as emperor, he eventually became a Christian and began the process of making Christianity the state religion.

Obviously some good resulted from Constantine's decision. The government no longer jailed, tortured, and killed Christians. The empire eventually ended slavery and protected human rights. Tragically, however, the power structure of the empire soon dominated the church. Over several centuries, the medieval Roman Catholic Church developed an elaborate system of penance that included belief in purgatory, the intercession of saints, and the power of the priest to absolve from the temporal punishment of sin.

In spite of all the developments away from the simplicity of the New Testament, we do owe considerable debt to the medieval church. It kept alive the gospel story. It preserved the manuscripts

Martin Luther

of the New Testament. Although corrupt in many ways, it was the church for centuries.

The Reformation

Even during the Middle Ages, some attempted to reform the church, with varying degrees of success. By the sixteenth century many more wanted reform, including Martin Luther (1483-1546), a German monk and theologian. The heart of his theology was justification by grace through faith, in contrast with the Roman Catholic practices of his day that implied people could merit salvation. Luther also called the church back to the authority of the Bible, wanting *sola scriptura*, "*Scripture alone*" as his guide. He never intended to form a new church, but eventually his followers were excommunicated by the Roman Catholic Church and formed a separate body.

John Calvin

In Switzerland, a more thoroughgoing Reformation took place under Huldreich Zwingli (1484-1531) at Zurich. Though his career was brief, Zwingli began the "Reformed" tradition, the second major Protestant movement after Lutheranism. John Calvin (1509-1564) in Geneva later became the chief influence in this Reformed Church. Calvin's emphasis on the sovereignty of God led him to emphasize the doctrine of predestination. This doctrine still shapes the churches of the Reformed tradition such as Presbyterians and many Baptists.

A third branch of the Reformation was the Anabaptist or Radical Reformation. Some considered these Christians "radical" because they insisted on a stricter return to the teaching of the New Testament, believing the pacifism Jesus taught on the Sermon on the Mount was crucial to a true Christian life. They also insisted on believer's baptism, thus earning themselves the name Anabaptists ("rebaptizers") from those who practiced infant baptism. This meant a break with the union of church and state that Constantine had established centuries before. Almost every government in

Anabaptist Martyrs

Europe, whether Catholic or Protestant, viewed their refusal to baptize infants as a threat to the social order. Consequently, Anabaptists faced severe persecution. Since most of them were pacifists, they refused to resist the government violently. Consequently, many fled to Holland where there was some degree of religious tolerance.

We in Christian Churches and Churches of Christ owe a great debt to the Reformation. Barton Stone, Alexander Campbell, and other leaders often praised Luther and Calvin for their work in leading people back to the Bible. Indeed, they saw their task as finishing the work of Reformation begun by Luther and others, often calling their work, "the Current Reformation."

England and Scotland

Since most of the early settlers in Britain's American colonies came from England and Scotland, the reformation in those countries had a more direct effect on the Stone-Campbell Movement in America. In England, prompted by personal, political, and religious problems, King Henry VIII (1491-1547) broke from the Roman Catholic Church in 1534 to form the Church of England. Of all the Reformation churches, this Anglican Church made the least changes from Catholic practices.

Consequently leaders arose who, influenced by the Reformed Church teaching of John Calvin, desired more reform in the Church of England. Their attempt to purify the church led to their being called Puritans. Some despaired of ever changing the Church of England and separated from it to form their own pure churches. These Separatists faced persecution in England and so some fled to Holland, then to America, becoming the Pilgrims of Plymouth Plantation.

Other Separatists organized themselves under groups of elders or presbyters. Through the leadership of John Knox (1513-1572) in Scotland, this Presbyterian system became the official Church of Scotland. Still other Separatists in England began to practice believer's immersion, and so became known as Baptists.

Members of all these groups—Anglicans, Puritans, Separatists, Presbyterians, and Baptists—eventually migrated to the English colonies in America. Thus, as we will see in the next chapter, the variety of churches in America soon led to a unique religious situation.

Enlightenment Rationalism

One of the consequences of the Protestant Reformation was a series of religious wars in Europe. The treaty that ended the bloody Thirty-Years War in 1648, the Peace of Westphalia, decreed that the religion of a country's ruler determined the religion of the country. There were Catholic countries and Protestant countries with little toleration of religious dissent. Consequently, wars over religion raged throughout Europe for decades. One result of the religious wars between Protestants and Catholics in Europe was the desire to have a more reasonable religion that would not lead to bloodshed. This desire was one cause of the

John Locke's writings on religious toleration greatly influenced leaders in the American churches as they formulated ideas of religious freedom and the primitive church.

Enlightenment era or Age of Reason in the 17th and 18th centuries. Some in this time rejected all religion as unreasonable. Others felt there was a religion based on the natural order that was reasonable, but that supernatural, miraculous religion was not. This group, generally known as Deists, redefined Christianity to remove the supernatural, miraculous elements.

Still others argued that supernatural Christianity was completely reasonable. The most influential of these thinkers was John Locke (1632-1704). Locke argued that all our ideas result from experience and that in light of that experience the essence of Christianity—Jesus as the Messiah—was completely reasonable. He did this by defining the supernatural as above reason but not contrary to it.

All of these forms of Enlightenment thought found their way to America. Deism influenced the founding Fathers, such as Thomas Jefferson who produced a New Testament without any miracle stories. More important to Christian Churches and Churches of Christ, our movement was born in an era when the rationalism of John Locke heavily influenced all of its early leaders.

This brief survey of church history before the colonization of America reminds us that we in Christian Churches and Churches of Christ are not the first Christians. As much as we might disagree with many of the individuals and churches mentioned in this chapter, we must admit they are in one sense our spiritual ancestors. With the light given them, many did their best throughout the ages to be faithful to Christ. The new religious situation in America, however, provided the soil for a more thoroughgoing reformation of the church, restoring certain items to the church that it had lost in this long history.

Questions for Discussion

1. What are some reasons we in Christian Churches and Churches of Christ have been reluctant to admit we have a history? Are these legitimate reasons?

2. What are the dangers in refusing to admit we have a history?

3. List some of the benefits of studying church history.

4. What is the difference between tradition and traditionalism? Give some biblical examples of the difference.

5. What are some of the spiritual debts we owe to the early church? The medieval church? The Reformation? What lessons can we learn today from the church in those times?

6. Is Christianity a "reasonable" religion? What are some of the dangers of making human reasonableness the test for the truths of Christianity?

For Further Reading

Allen, C. Leonard and Hughes, Richard T. *Discovering our Roots: The Ancestry of Churches of Christ*. Abilene, TX: ACU Press, 1988.

Garrett, Leroy. *The Stone-Campbell Movement*. Joplin, MO: College Press, 1994. See Pages 21-45.

Gonzalez, Justo L. *The Story of Christianity*. Peabody, MA: Prince Press, 1999.

The Promise of Restoration in Early America

Why is religion in America different from religion in Europe and the rest of the world? Why is it, even today, that there are more denominations in America than in the rest of the world? Why is the percentage of regular church-goers higher in America? Why do Americans tend to take religion so seriously?

We find the answer to all these questions in the early history of America. That history also is the soil that gave birth to the Christian Churches and Churches of Christ in America. Although most of the early colonies had established tax-supported religions, a new situation developed in Colonial America that had never existed before. No single religious group became dominant over all the colonies. The Puritans dominated New England, but there were also Baptists and Anglicans there. The Anglicans were most numerous in the southern colonies, but there were also Presbyterians and Methodists. The middle colonies had the greatest religious diversity with Quakers, Lutherans, German Reformed, Baptists, Anglicans, and others.

Consequently, no one denomination could be the church of America. We take that situation for granted, but it was unique for its time. In Europe, every country had an official state religion, with (at best) limited tolerance for other religious groups. For example, English authorities jailed the Separatist Puritans we call the "Pilgrims" for preaching against the Church of England. Therefore, they left England for the Netherlands and eventually came to America, not to find the religious freedom we have today, but to have the freedom to set up "the true church." They were no more tolerant of Quakers and Baptists than the English authorities had been tolerant of Puritans.

A New View of Religious Freedom

Since no religious group dominated all the colonies, a new form of religious freedom began in America. It was a freedom from church or clerical authority. Many Americans, especially on the frontier, wanted no part of a Pope, a bishop, or even a group of clergy making rules for the church. Instead, they longed for a more democratic form of government where ordinary members made collective decisions for the church. This desire for religious democracy also produced a new form of minister—one who was not formally educated, but who came from the people—in contrast to the old elite, educated ministry.

American religious freedom was also a freedom from tradition. The common sense of the people replaced the rulings of Popes and councils, the historic creeds, and the writings of educated theologians. The people should read the Bible for themselves and think for themselves, not trust the clergy to do their thinking for them.

Because of this democratization of Christianity, another freedom arose—the freedom to begin new churches. What happened if your reading of Scripture differed significantly from the teaching of your church? If you could not persuade your church to change, then there was no choice left but to form your own "true" church. As a result, dozens of upstart churches began or prospered in America, the Baptists and Methodists in particular, many outgrowing the more established churches. After a while those newer churches themselves resisted change in their practices and grew to be leaders in the larger culture. Consequently, some in those groups rebelled against their tradition and formed still other religious sects.

A New View of Religious Authority

Because of this freedom, many thought it no longer necessary for religious authority to come from a recognized hierarchy, creeds, and educated clergy. Christianity became truly democratic, a rule of the people. The Reformation principle of *sola scriptura* (Scripture alone) evolved into the idea that every Christian had the right to interpret the Bible for himself or herself.

Of course this interpretation was done rationally and with common sense. Reason was to judge the truth of any religious teaching. Increasingly, this meant that each individual had the right and responsibility to read Scripture and interpret it. However, personal experience shaped this rationalism, particularly on the American frontier. In other words, true religion was to be heartfelt and mysterious, while at the same time being reasonable to the average person.

Ironically, this rejection of traditional religious authorities gave power to another elite, that is, religious demagogues. Although theoretically, each person was a Bible interpreter, in fact a religious leader who could move an audience had tremendous influence on how that audience understood Scripture. This accounts for the rise of popular preaching in the language of the people. It also explains the popularity of the new religious press. By publishing a paper, preachers could move thousands to see the Bible and the church their way.

What was the result of this shift of power from traditional religious authorities to popular preachers? Unfortunately, the church became less unified. Mass movements and denominations multiplied. For some popularity equaled truth. Too often, freedom to follow Scripture for one's self gave way to bondage to self promoting preachers whose success was measured in terms of numbers, not faithfulness.

A Call for Restoration

This was the setting for the birth of Christian Churches and Churches of Christ. Many were looking for a more certain authority in religion. Many wondered why there were so many denominations and which (if any) was the true church. The scandal of division among Christians was evident on the frontier. A small settlement of a hundred people might have three or more struggling churches, often in constant conflict with each other over who was the true, correct church.

But the frontier also offered many religious leaders the freedom to rethink the shape of the church. Independently, many of them decided that a return to the Bible and the church of the New

Testament offered the best hope of having a faithful and a unified church in their new American setting. These "back to the Bible" movements grew up in several denominations in various parts of the frontier.

As we saw in chapter one, the dream of going "back to the Bible" did not begin in eighteenth century America. The Renaissance call to go "back to the sources" led many like the Roman Catholic scholar Erasmus (1466-1536) to emphasize the importance of going to the New Testament for guidance and authority. The Reformation had its motto of *sola scriptura*, Scripture alone. The Puritans in England and the early New England colonies wanted their churches to resemble closely the biblical model. However, on the eighteenth century American frontier, many called for a more thorough reformation of the church. Some used the word "restoration" for this reform.

"Restoration" was a more popular term in the Campbell Movement (see chapter four) than in the early movements examined in this chapter, but the concept of restoration was common to all these groups. What did they mean by a "Restoration Movement"?

Some thought of restoration in terms of restoring a house. Restoring the church was not building from scratch; it's not as though the church had completely disappeared, but it had deteriorated through the years and needed to be restored to its original state. Think of restoring an old house. Essential portions of the house may be sound and original—the foundation and plumbing, for example—while other portions need replacing. Restoration means removing newer additions and rebuilding older sections in order to return the house to its original condition.

This was the goal of all the groups in this chapter. What most also had in common was agreement on the purpose of restoration. To be the pure church of the Bible was not an end in itself. The purpose of restoring the church was to reach the unity among Christians that Christ prayed for, "That all of them may be one…" (John 17:21). Although there were significant differences among these groups, they all called Christians back to the Bible to restore to the church certain things they believed it had lost.

Christians of the South: James O'Kelly

"I am for Bible government, Christian equality, and the Christian name." So said James O'Kelly (1735-1826), an early Methodist preacher in North Carolina and Virginia. When the Methodist church in America organized itself in Baltimore in 1784, O'Kelly and a few other ministers questioned the appointment of Francis Asbury as one of two superintendents of the church. They believed Asbury, who began to call himself bishop, held too much power over the churches. Eventually, O'Kelly not only opposed Asbury but the whole idea of a bishop who appoints ministers in each church. Instead, he felt each congregation should act democratically, like a republic, to govern its own affairs.

In 1793, O'Kelly and others broke from Asbury's leadership, calling themselves Republican Methodists. In August 1794, the leaders of this group met and went one step farther. They decided

James O'Kelly

to call themselves "Christians" to the exclusion of other names and take the Bible alone as their creed.

Eventually, they adopted six "Cardinal Principles of the Christian Church."

1. The Lord Jesus Christ is the only Head of the Church.
2. The name Christian should be used to the exclusion of all party and sectarian names.
3. The Holy Bible, or Scriptures of the Old and New Testaments, is our only creed, and a sufficient rule of faith and practice.
4. Christian character, or vital piety, is the only test of church fellowship and membership.
5. The right of private judgment and the liberty of conscience are the privilege and duty of all.
6. The union of all followers of Christ to the end that the world may believe.

Circuit Rider

These leaders did not intend these items as a formal creed (since item three rejects creeds), but these propositions do express the basic outlook of the O'Kelly group and of all the restoration movements on the frontier. Note that even Christian unity was not an end in itself, but should result in the evangelization of the world.

These Christian churches eventually numbered 10,000 or so members in North Carolina and Virginia. Some of these congregations eventually adopted believer's immersion and united with the New England Christians in the early 1800's (see below). Others maintained infant baptism and rejoined the Methodists in 1934. Others joined with the Stone "Christians" (see chapter three). One connection between the O'Kelly and the Stone Movements was the work of Rice Haggard (1769-1819) who convinced both groups to take the name "Christian" to the exclusion of other divisive names.

The New England Christian Connection: Jones and Smith

Independently a similar movement arose among Baptists in New England. At this time, Baptists were strongly Calvinistic, believing in predestination. Abner Jones (1772-1841), a physician and preacher in Vermont joined with like-minded Baptists in denying Calvinism and taking the name Christian. They organized a Christian church in Lyndon, Vermont, in 1801. Jones became a traveling evangelist, spreading the message of non-creedal Christianity.

In 1803, Jones first met Elias Smith (1769-1846), another Baptist minister who had formed a Christian congregation the previous year in Portsmouth, New Hampshire. Smith was a fiery proponent of religious freedom who published one of the earliest Christian papers in America, the *Herald of Gospel Liberty* (begun in 1808). He also popularized his ideas through hymns that attacked the prevailing religious authorities. Jones and Smith combined their efforts and by 1807 had established fourteen congregations of Christians in New England.

The Smith-Jones Movement was so insistent on doctrinal diversity that eventually it splintered and disappeared as a separate

Elias Smith

fellowship. Some became Unitarians. Many later joined the Adventists. Some joined with the O'Kelly Christians in the South and the Stone Movement to form the Christian Connection. In 1931, the congregations of the Connection that had not merged with the Campbell Movement in the nineteenth century became part of the Congregational Christian Church which in turn merged with the Evangelical and Reformed Church to form the United Church of Christ in 1957.

The freedom of the frontier thus produced two Christian "restoration" movements, one from the Methodists and one from the Baptists. It was to produce two more from a Presbyterian background.

Questions for Discussion

1. What factors led to religious freedom in America? How does that freedom help explain the unique aspects of American religion?

2. Why are there so many different churches in America? Why have new religious groups been so popular in the United States?

3. What do you first think of when you hear "Restoration Movement"? How have many in Christian Churches and Churches of Christ understood restoration? How should we understand it?

4. Is Christian unity still a noble goal to pursue? What would that unity look like?

5. Are the "six points" of the O'Kelly Christians a good summary of what the church should be? What would you add or subtract from their list?

6. What did the Smith-Jones New England Christians and the O'Kelly Christians have in common? How were they different? What can we learn today from these two groups?

For Further Reading:

Conkin, Paul K. *American Originals*. Chapel Hill: University of North Carolina Press, 1997. See Pages 1-8.

Garrett, Leroy. *The Stone-Campbell Movement*. Joplin, Missouri: College Press, 1994. See Pages 47-70.

Hatch, Nathan O. "The Christian Movement and the Demand for a Theology of the People," in *American Origins of Churches of Christ*. Abilene: ACU Press, 2000. See Pages 11-44.

Hatch, Nathan O. *The Democratization of American Christianity*. New Haven: Yale University Press, 1989.

McAllister, Lester G. and Tucker, William E. *Journey in Faith*. Saint Louis, Chalice Press, 1975. See Pages 51-60.

North, James B. *Union in Truth: An Interpretive History of the Restoration Movement*. Cincinnati: Standard Publishing, 1994. See pages 1-32.

West, Earl Irvin. *The Search for the Ancient Order*, Vol. 1. Nashville: Gospel Advocate, 1986. See pages 1-17.

Barton Stone and Christian Unity

Although there were groups of "Christians" in the South and in New England, the most numerous band grew out of the Presbyterian and Baptist churches in Kentucky and Tennessee. The leader of these "Christians of the West" was a deeply spiritual man named Barton W. Stone.

Stone's Early Life

Barton W. Stone (1772-1844) was born in Maryland and raised as a nominal Episcopalian. In 1779, after the death of his father, Stone moved with his family to Virginia. During his teen years, he attended Baptist and Methodist churches, but could not experience the kind of dramatic conversion some did. Instead, he decided to improve his position in society by continuing his education and becoming a lawyer.

He enrolled in a "log college" (a typical, one-teacher frontier school) run by David Caldwell (1725-1824), a Presbyterian minister in North Carolina. Under his influence and the preaching of revivalist James McGready (1760-1817), Stone had a conversion experience, became a Presbyterian, and felt the call to preach. Finishing his studies with Caldwell in three years, Stone was one of the most educated persons on the American frontier.

Stone had many internal struggles before he was ordained as a Presbyterian minister. He questioned the depth of his conversion, the genuineness of his call to preach, and the truth of the traditional doctrines of the Trinity and predestination. He believed so strongly in the

Barton W. Stone

reality of but one God, that the idea of the Trinity even disrupted his prayer life. For a while he taught at a Methodist school in Georgia, but soon made a trek across Tennessee and Kentucky in 1796, preaching and searching for God's will for his life.

Stone eventually concluded God had called him to preach and so sought ordination from the Transylvania Presbytery at Cane Ridge, Kentucky, where he had been preaching for two years. He still had serious doubts about the doctrine of the Trinity found in the Westminster Confession of Faith (the basic creed of the Presbyterians). Agreement with this Presbyterian confession was required for ordination. After some discussion with the presbytery, he was asked if he would adopt the Confession of Faith. He replied, " I do, as far as I see it consistent with the word of God." This reply was common among those trained in the revival tradition in Presbyterianism, and so satisfied the presbytery. Thus Stone was ordained and assigned to minister to the churches at Cane Ridge and Concord, Kentucky, in 1798.

The Cane Ridge Revival

In August 1801, Cane Ridge was the site of the largest and most famous camp meeting revival in American history. A wave of revivals led by James McGready and others had broken out in southern Kentucky in 1800. At the Cane Ridge revival, crowds estimated from 10,000 to 30,000 heard Baptist, Methodist, and Presbyterian ministers preach repentance. During their preaching, many listeners experienced what Stone and others called "religious exercises." Some fell to the ground in a faint as if they were dead. Some jerked back and forth and made a sound like a bark. Others felt bodily agitation coming upon them and tried to run away. Some danced back and forth in place. A few laughed a hearty, solemn laugh.

How should we understand these experiences—falling, jerks, barks, running, dancing, laughing? All his life Barton Stone believed they were evidence of the Holy Spirit working through the unusual circumstances of the times. In his autobiography he says that the truly strange thing would have been if these " exercises" had not occurred, given the feeling by many that the end of the world was near. Does Stone's seeing this Spirit at work in the lives of people affected by these experiences make him Pentecostal or Charismatic? No. While he thought the Spirit could work in any circumstances to convict people of their sin, he never thought that these extreme events were meant to be the universal experience of all Christians. In other words, although the Spirit may work in such dramatic circumstances on some believers, one can be a mature, faithful Christian through the power of the Spirit without these unusual spiritual exercises. To call him Pentecostal or Charismatic would be inaccurate and anachronistic.

Still, the Cane Ridge Revival had a profound effect on Stone and others. It convinced them of the importance of Christian unity. If the Spirit could come in response to Baptist, Methodist, and Presbyterian preaching, then the differences between these denominations must not be matters of the gospel. The unity among Christians produced by the Spirit should be a goal of all who claim to follow Christ. In Stone's words, "Let Christian unity be our polar star."

The experiences of Cane Ridge also increased the doubts that Stone and his fellow ministers had about Calvinistic predestination. Although one can be a Calvinist and a revivalist, they had seen many freely respond to the gospel and the Spirit during the revivals. They felt more at home with a doctrine of limited but real free will.

The shrine protecting the Cane Ridge Meeting House

THE LAST WILL AND TESTAMENT

This desire for unity soon proved itself in concrete action. The Presbyterian Synod of Kentucky questioned Stone and five other ministers about their support of the revival, their more open stance toward other Christians, and their doubts about Calvinism. Before the Synod could discipline them, they broke away and formed their own association, the Springfield Presbytery. Within a year, they decided the Springfield Presbytery itself worked against biblical unity so they decided to disband. They gave their reasons for doing so in *The Last Will and Testament of the Springfield Presbytery* written in 1804. This document is so significant in our history that we give it in its entirety (including its nineteenth century grammar and style):

The PRESBYTERY OF SPRINGFIELD, sitting at Caneridge, in the county of Bourbon, being, through a gracious Providence, in more than ordinary bodily health, growing in strength and size daily; and in perfect soundness and composure of mind; but knowing that it is appointed for all delegated bodies once to die: and considering that the life of every such body is very uncertain, do make, and ordain this our Last Will and Testament, in manner and form following, viz.:

> *Imprimis.* We *will*, that this body die, be dissolved, and sink into union with the Body of Christ at large; for there is but one body, and one spirit, even as we are called in one hope of our calling.
>
> *Item.* We *will*, that our name of distinction, with its *Reverend* title, be forgotten, that there be but one Lord over God's heritage, and his name one.
>
> *Item.* We *will*, that our power of making laws for the government of the church, and executing them by delegated authority, forever cease; that the people may have free course to the Bible, and adopt *the law of the spirit of life in Christ Jesus.*

Item. We *will*, that candidates for the Gospel ministry henceforth study the Holy Scriptures with fervent prayer, and obtain license from God to preach the simple Gospel, *with the Holy Ghost sent down from heaven*, without any mixture of philosophy, vain deceit, traditions of men, or the rudiments of the world. And let none henceforth take *this honor to himself, but he that is called of God, as was Aaron.*

Item. We *will*, that the church of Christ assume her native right of internal government—try her candidates for the ministry, as to their soundness in the faith, acquaintance with experimental religion, gravity and aptness to teach; and admit no other proof of their authority but Christ speaking in them. We will that the church of Christ look up to the Lord of the harvest to send forth laborers into his harvest; and that she resume her primitive right of trying those who say they are Apostles, and are not.

Item. We *will*, that each particular church, as a body, actuated by the same spirit, choose her own preacher, and support him by a free will offering, without written call or *subscription*—admit members—remove offenses; and never henceforth *delegate* her right of government to any man or set of men whatever.

Item. We *will*, that the people henceforth take the Bible as the only sure guide to heaven; and as many as are offended with other books, which stand in competition with it, may cast them into the fire if they choose: for it is better to enter into life having one book, than having many to be cast into hell.

Item. We *will*, that preachers and people, cultivate a spirit of mutual forbearance; pray more and dispute less; and while they behold the signs of the times, look up, and confidently expect that redemption draweth nigh.

Item. We *will*, that our weak brethren, who may have been wishing to make the Presbytery of Springfield their king, and wot not what is now become of it, betake themselves to the Rock of Ages, and follow Jesus for the future.

Item. We *will*, that the Synod of Kentucky examine every member, who may be *suspected* of having departed from the

> Confession of Faith, and suspend every such suspected heretic immediately; in order that the oppressed may go free, and taste the sweets of gospel liberty.
>
> *Item.* We *will*, that Ja— , the author of two letters lately published in Lexington, be encouraged in his zeal to destroy *partyism*. We will, moreover, that our past conduct be examined into by all who may have correct information; but let foreigners beware of speaking evil of things which they know not.
>
> *Item.* Finally we *will*, that all our *sister bodies* read their Bibles carefully, that they may see their fate there determined, and prepare for death before it is too late.

Signed by Stone and five other ministers, this was a clear call for restoration and unity. Much of this document still has great influence on Christian Churches and Churches of Christ. Some items deserve to have more influence on us. Christians should follow the Bible alone. Each local congregation should run its own affairs and choose its own ministers, who are to be ordained with certain authority and responsibility, but not to be rule-making "reverends." There should be no formal organization beyond the local church, such as a presbytery of ministers. A spirit of cooperation and freedom should prevail. We should dispute less, and instead prayerfully look forward to the redemption Christ brings at his Second Coming.

The Growth of the Stone Movement

At the suggestion of Rice Haggard, a former associate of James O'Kelly, Stone and his followers soon called themselves Christians and established congregations they called Churches of Christ or Christian Churches. By 1807, the question of baptism arose in the movement. Eventually the Stone churches practiced believer's immersion but did not make it an absolute test of fellowship (those only baptized as infants could still be members and commune). Stone feared that making believer's immersion a test of fellowship would exclude more Christians than any creed.

Stone faced vehement opposition to two of his theological positions. He denied the substitutionary view of the atonement, the idea that Christ paid our debt to God on the cross. To Stone, such a view made God a hateful tyrant demanding payment instead of a loving Father. He also would not affirm the traditional doctrine of the Trinity, although he did praise Jesus as the Son of God. On these issues, Stone insisted on the literal wording of the Bible, accusing others of speculative theology.

Yet in spite of Stone's theological opponents, the defection of some leaders to the Shakers, and the return of others to the Presbyterians, by the 1820's the Stone Movement had grown to 12,000 members and spread from Kentucky and Ohio to Tennessee, Alabama, Missouri, and Illinois. A great deal of this growth was due to whole congregations of Separate Baptists giving up their "Baptist" name to be "Christians."

This growth was also the result of the example and character of Barton W. Stone. Not only was he a tireless evangelist himself, but his peaceful spirit and love for the lost influenced others through his paper, *The Christian Messenger* (published 1826-1844). Although Stone continued to discuss his objections to substitutionary atonement and traditional Trinitarianism in his paper, he focused more often on Christian tolerance and unity. Soon he would make his unity teaching concrete by combining his movement with one led by Thomas and Alexander Campbell.

Thus by 1804 three American independent movements were attempting to be "Christians only." Although there were differences among them, having come from three different denominations—Methodists, Baptists, and Presbyterians—their similarities are striking. All three wanted the Bible alone to be their creed. All took the name "Christian." All organized themselves congregationally, without the control of a bishop or a clergy-led presbytery. Each worked to promote Christian unity. All were evangelistic. These "restoration movements" were to have a lasting heritage in America.

Questions for Discussion

1. What do you think about the "spiritual exercises" at the Cane Ridge Revival? Were these genuine experiences of the Holy Spirit, or should they be explained another way? Is there room in Christian Churches and Churches of Christ for such experiences today? Should there be?

2. List and discuss at least five themes found in *The Last Will and Testament of the Springfield Presbytery* that still influence Christian Churches and Churches of Christ. What else can we learn from this document to help our current spiritual walk?

3. Why might Stone object to the idea of substitutionary atonement, that Jesus paid our debt of sin to alleviate God's anger toward us? What does this doctrine imply about God?

4. How important is the doctrine of the Trinity? How important has it been in Christian Churches and Churches of Christ?

5. What are the similarities and differences among the three "Christian" groups we have discussed so far?

For Further Reading

Conkin, Paul K. *American Originals*. Chapel Hill: University of North Carolina Press, 1997. See Pages 8-14.

Garrett, Leroy. *The Stone-Campbell Movement*. Joplin, Missouri: College Press, 1994. See Pages 71-95.

McAllister, Lester G. and Tucker, William E. *Journey in Faith*. Saint Louis, Chalice Press, 1975. See Pages 61-88.

North, James B. *Union in Truth: An Interpretive History of the Restoration Movement*. Cincinnati: Standard Publishing, 1994. See pages 33-70.

Webb, Henry E. *In Search of Christian Unity: A History of the Restoration Movement*, revised edition. Abilene, TX: ACU Press, 2003. See Pages 41-59.

West, Earl Irvin. *The Search for the Ancient Order*, Vol. 1. Nashville: Gospel Advocate, 1986. See pages 18-35.

Williams, D. Newell. *Barton Stone, A Spiritual Biography*. St Louis: Chalice Press, 2000.

The Coming of the Campbells

While O'Kelly, Smith, Jones, and Stone were forming Christian groups in America, Thomas Campbell (1763-1854) was still in Ireland. The religious pilgrimage of the Campbell family is interesting. Thomas's father, Archibald Campbell, was an Anglican converted from Roman Catholicism. Thomas converted to the Presbyterian Church of Scotland, becoming a minister for the Ahorey Church in Rich Hill, Ireland.

While in Ireland, Thomas Campbell became dissatisfied with the narrowness of the Old Light, Anti-Burgher, Seceder Presbyterian Church to which he belonged. Each of these terms denoted a previous doctrinal split among the Presbyterians. Campbell longed instead for the unity that the early church enjoyed and even made several unsuccessful attempts to unite the different factions in the Seceder Church in Ireland.

Rich Hill Ireland Church

In 1807, Thomas came to America, leaving his family behind in Ireland to join him later. Assigned to preach in Western Pennsylvania, Campbell soon was in trouble for allowing Presbyterians of all stripes to take the Lord's Supper. Censured by his presbytery and synod, Campbell began an inter-denominational Bible study group, patterned on British missionary and Bible societies, known as the Christian Association of Washington, Pennsylvania.

Thomas Campbell

The Declaration and Address

In 1809, the Christian Association commissioned Thomas Campbell to write a document outlining the purpose of the organization and its plan for unity among Christians. This *Declaration and Address* (a reference to the freedom proclaimed by the American *Declaration of Independence*) made a clear call back to the freedom found in the New Testament as a basis for Christian unity.

One can get lost in the 19th century language of the *Declaration and Address*, but its main points include:

1. *A fervent call to Christian unity.* "That the Church of Christ on earth is essentially, intentionally, and constitutionally one." It is one in essence because Christians are "subjects of the same grace, objects of the same divine love, bought with the same price, and joint heirs of the same inheritance." God intends the church to be one, evidenced by Jesus' fervent prayer for unity in John 17. The "constitution" that makes the church one is the New Testament.
2. *A strong condemnation of division among Christians.* "That division among Christians is a horrid evil, fraught with many evils." Thus, there should "be no schisms, no uncharitable divisions among them."
3. *Doctrinal differences not based on the express teachings of the New Testament are the causes of division.* More than sixty times in the *Declaration and Address*, Campbell uses phrases like "expressly exhibited," "plain," and "clear" to describe the binding teachings of Scripture. Where the Bible is unclear or silent, no disagreement should divide Christians. Thomas Campbell never spelled out exactly what those "express teachings" are. Neither does he address the difficulty of Christians strongly disagreeing over what the Bible "expressly" teaches. This would be a significant problem later in the Campbell Movement.
4. *A simple confession of faith in Jesus, not agreement with an elaborate creed, is all that is necessary for admission to the*

church. Thus, creeds, even if true and helpful, should not be used to exclude Christians who disagree with them from full acceptance as children of God.

5. *A desire to return to the purity of the first century church*. By removing items that have divided Christians and obscured the beauty of the church, God's people can experience personal and corporate holiness and purity.
6. *An appeal for love and understanding among Christians*. Those who confess faith in Christ "should consider each other as the precious saints of God, should love each other as brethren, children of the same family and Father, temples of the same Spirit, members of the same body…"

Thomas Campbell never intended the principles of the *Declaration and Address* to be the basis of a new religious group. Instead, it was a call to unity among Christians of all denominations. "The cause that we advocate is not our own peculiar cause, nor the cause of any party, considered as such; it is a common cause, the cause of Christ and our brethren of all denominations."

Things changed when the Christian Association of Washington eventually formed the nucleus of a new congregation, the Brush Run church. By forming a church, Campbell made his quest for Christian unity more difficult. Even today, in a Bible study group with people from different denominations, it seems as if we have so much in common. Why can't we unite? But if that Bible study group were to become a church, then they would have to make certain decisions that would highlight the differences among them. How will they worship? Who will lead them? Who can be a part of this church? What does the church believe and teach? It is easier to talk about unity than to actually achieve it.

Having said this, we don't want to diminish the power of Thomas Campbell's call to Christian unity. As we will see in later chapters, Christian Churches and Churches of Christ eventually neglected this unity theme. The *Declaration and Address* reminds us that if we are to be biblical we must take Christ's prayer for unity more seriously than we have.

Alexander Campbell in Scotland

The rest of Thomas Campbell's family, including his oldest son Alexander (1788-1866), soon boarded a ship from Ireland to join him in America. Storms shipwrecked it off the coast of Scotland. Consequently, the family spent close to a year in Glasgow, 1808-1809, allowing Alexander to attend classes at the university there.

Robert Sandeman

While in Glasgow, Alexander made friends with Greville Ewing and others who had broken from the Church of Scotland and formed independent churches. Ewing was associated with two brothers, James and Robert Haldane, who in turn were influenced by the thought of John Glas and Robert Sandeman. Glas, Sandeman, the Haldanes, and Ewing all wished to unify Christians and return to the practices of the New Testament church. Although they did not agree on every detail, these practices included local church leadership by elders, weekly Lord's Supper, Love Feasts with footwashing and the holy kiss, believer's baptism by immersion, opposition to ministerial titles such as "Reverend," and separation of church and state.

During his stay in Glasgow, Alexander never joined any of these independent churches, but he became increasingly dissatisfied with what he perceived as the narrowness of the Seceder Presbyterians. One of his last acts in Scotland before the family finally sailed successfully to America was to refuse quietly to commune with the Seceder church.

Father and Son Reunion

After landing in New York, the family reunited in Western Pennsylvania in October 1809. Both Thomas and Alexander told of their separate difficulties with the Seceder Presbyterian Church. Alexander read a proof copy of the *Declaration and Address* and

Alexander Campbell

pledged to devote his life to promoting the principles he found there. Alexander began to study for the ministry under his father, and when the Brush Run church began in 1811, both father and son did their share of the preaching.

Also in 1811, Alexander married Margaret Brown, the daughter of a farmer who lived just over the line in what now is West Virginia. They lived on her father's farm until he eventually deeded the property to them. This property in what became Bethany, West Virginia, was to be the home of Alexander Campbell and the center of the movement he led until his death.

A year after their marriage, Margaret and Alexander had their first child, Jane. The birth of Jane was more than a time of joy for the family; it also was a theological crisis. Some in the Brush Run Church had questioned the validity of their infant baptism and requested immersion as adults. Thus, Alexander Campbell faced a decision. Should he baptize his infant daughter? Should he himself be baptized? After months of study, he concluded that biblical baptism was immersion of believers, not sprinkling of infants. In June 1812, Matthias Luce, a Baptist minister, baptized Alexander and Thomas Campbell along with their wives and three others from the Brush Run Church.

Soon most of the members at Brush Run were immersed as believers. This further separated the Campbells from their Presbyterian roots, since Presbyterians believed they should baptize infants for several reasons, particularly to cleanse them from the sin they inherited from Adam. On the other hand, the practice of believer's immersion brought the Campbells into the orbit of the Baptists on the frontier. After much discussion, the Brush Run Church joined the Redstone Baptist Association in 1815.

Reformers Among the Baptists

Joining the Redstone Baptist Association might look like an abandonment of the Campbells' goal to unite all Christians. How could they call for Christian unity when they belonged to a particular denomination? The Campbells, however, especially Thomas, did not see things that way. Instead, he felt that any visible unity was a step toward the ultimate unity of Christians. It was better to be part of a Baptist Association than to be solely an individual congregation.

For the next fifteen years, the Campbells were reformers among the Baptists. Soon their followers planted new congregations in addition to the Brush Run Church. Alexander Campbell became influential through his work as an educator, publisher and debater. From 1818-1823 he educated young men for the ministry in his home. In 1823, he began a monthly periodical, the *Christian Baptist*. The tone of the paper was iconoclastic, attacking traditional institutions, particularly the power of the clergy. Alexander was determined to tear down every practice that stood in the way of restoring New Testament Christianity and the unity of the early church.

Although teaching and writing gave him some notoriety, his debating made Alexander Campbell a household name on the frontier. The Campbells had opposed disputes and debates as antithetical to Christian unity. But religious and political debating was a common practice in early America. After the Baptists approached him several times to defend believer's immersion in debate, Alexander finally agreed. In 1820, he faced John Walker and in 1823, William Maccalla, each Presbyterian ministers who argued for infant baptism. These debates, especially in their printed forms, were widely influential and convinced even Thomas Campbell that debating could be a positive way to advance the cause of restoration and unity.

Although his debates made him the champion of believer's immersion, other teachings made Campbell suspect among many of the Baptists. As early as 1816, he offended a number of Baptist leaders with his "Sermon on the Law" delivered to the meeting of the Redstone Association. In the sermon, Campbell made a sharp distinction between the Old and New Testaments, arguing that the Law of Moses was not authoritative for determining the beliefs and actions of the church. Strong opposition from certain ministers in the Redstone Association led Campbell to transfer his membership to a congregation in the nearby Mahoning Baptist Association, a group more favorable to Campbell's reforms. The churches of the Mahoning Association grew significantly due to the evangelism of Walter Scott (see chapter six). Jealousy of that growth and the increasing realization that the Campbells did not accept Baptist beliefs concerning such things as the meaning of baptism and the role of the minister soon caused other Baptist Associations to turn against them. Campbell had increasingly understood baptism to be the place where God forgives sin and moves the person into the kingdom. He became stronger in his antagonism toward clergy the longer he dealt with what he considered tyrannical Baptist ministers. Eventually, Campbell and others decided they could no longer be reformers within the Baptist Church. Consequently, the Mahoning Association dissolved itself in 1830, followed by numerous Baptist Associations throughout Virginia, Ohio, and adjacent states that also dissolved or divided, following the lead of the Campbells.

Disciples of Christ

Now an independent movement, the churches led by Campbell faced the question of what to call themselves. Many individual followers preferred the name "Christian." Congregations often called themselves by a community name, "the Brush Run Church" or the "Wellsburg church." Sometimes a sign on the outside of the building read, "Church of Christ" or "Christian Church."

This confusion of names was in many ways intentional. They did not want an exclusive sectarian or denominational name. They wanted to call all followers of Jesus to unity. Nevertheless, one name increasingly characterized this congregationally organized church—Disciples of Christ. Alexander Campbell particularly preferred this name to "Christian." After all, the followers of Jesus were called Disciples before they were called Christians. He also was somewhat nervous about having his movement confused with the Christian movements of New England and Virginia or even the Christian movement led by Barton Stone.

Yet, the similarities between these Disciples and the Stone Christians were so obvious that the two groups would eventually unite, although without the strong support of Alexander Campbell. The next chapter tells that part of the story.

Questions for Discussion

1. Briefly describe Thomas Campbell's plan for producing Christian unity. What parts of that plan seem least workable? What parts do we need to emphasize today?

2. Would it have been better if Thomas Campbell had not started a church but had continued to work in an interdenominational Bible study? Can one be a Christian without belonging to a local church?

3. How did the church leaders he met in Scotland affect the ideas Alexander Campbell later had about the church?

4. What are the ways Alexander Campbell spread his ideas among the Baptists?

5. Why did the Campbells eventually leave the Baptist Association?

6. Why did Alexander Campbell prefer the name "Disciple"?

For Further Reading

Conkin, Paul K. *American Originals*. Chapel Hill: University of North Carolina Press, 1997. See Pages 14-22.

Garrett, Leroy. *The Stone-Campbell Movement*. Joplin, Missouri: College Press, 1994. See Pages 97-141.

Hughes, Richard T. *The Churches of Christ*. Westport, Connecticut: Praeger Press, 2001. See Pages 3-98.

McAllister, Lester G. and Tucker, William E. *Journey in Faith*. Saint Louis, Missouri: Chalice Press, 1975. See Pages 89-146.

North, James B. *Union in Truth: An Interpretive History of the Restoration Movement*. Cincinnati: Standard Publishing, 1994. See pages 71-152.

Olbricht, Thomas H. and Rollmann, Hans. *The Quest for Christian Unity, Peace, and Purity in Thomas Campbell's Declaration and Address*. Lanham, Maryland: Scarecrow Press, 2000.

Webb, Henry E. *In Search of Christian Unity*. Abilene, Texas: Abilene Christian University Press, 2001.

West, Earl Irvin. *The Search for the Ancient Order*, Vol. 1. Nashville: Gospel Advocate, 1986. See pages 36-75.

The Stone and Campbell Movements Unite

Take a map of the United States in 1820 and begin drawing concentric circles around the Stone Movement's strongholds. Do the same for the Campbell Movement, and you will see the circles begin to intersect in western Virginia, Ohio, and Kentucky. Especially in these last two states, members of the two groups were increasingly in close contact with one another. In many towns, like Georgetown and Lexington, Kentucky, there were congregations of each group.

Bethany Church

Alexander Campbell first visited Kentucky in 1823, and the next year he met Stone in the living room of Stone's Georgetown home. The two sensed a close kinship of ideas and goals and expressed great respect for one another. Later in life, Stone said there were fewer faults in Campbell than in any man he knew, acknowledging that Campbell was the greatest promoter of the religious reformation in which they both were involved. In Stone's obituary notice in the 1844 *Millennial Harbinger*, Campbell hailed Stone as the instrument of bringing many out of human tradition to accept the Bible as their confession of faith and rule of life.

Comparing the Men and Their Movements

Yet Campbell and Stone always regarded each other with a bit of uneasiness. Certainly there were educational and economic differences between the two. Campbell was a wealthy farmer and landowner while Stone often lived near the edge of poverty. Campbell had studied at the University of Glasgow while Stone trained at a frontier academy and on-the-job. They were different personalities in many ways. It was something else, though, that gave an edge to their relationship.

Stone believed that the bottom line of this religious reformation was to create lives characterized by the spirit of Christ. The love, humility, patience, and joy described as the fruit of the Spirit were the ultimate goals—the real tests of success. He sought to nurture these foundational traits by freeing people from the shackles of creeds and denominational structures to rely on the Bible alone. Only when believers embodied those virtues could Christians unite and true reform come. He regarded Alexander Campbell as too rigid on certain doctrines resulting in a de-emphasis on the work of the Holy Spirit.

Campbell, on the other hand, thought that Stone and the other "Christian" groups were too lax on doctrine. The New England Christians especially were quite unorthodox in their views of the Trinity and the work of Christ. Some even taught universalism—that God would eventually save all people. Campbell's platform for reform was to return to the ancient gospel and order of things—the doctrines and practices of the early church. He certainly believed that true submission to Christ would result in the fruits of the Spirit so important to Stone. But Campbell believed restoring the doctrinal details seen in the New Testament would reform the church and bring Christian unity.

They had so much in common, though. They were committed to the Scriptures as the only true source of spiritual light, life, and authority. They were committed to ending the shameful divisions among followers of Christ, and therefore opposed anything that separated Christians including creeds, clergy, unscriptural names, and denominational bodies. They believed that the church depicted in the New Testament was the ideal church, pure and free from all the corruption of the ages. Restoring that unified church was the goal.

Early Moves Toward Union and Difficulties

As early as the 1820s, members of the two bodies began asking why they weren't one. In August 1831, Stone replied to the question in his paper the *Christian Messenger*. As far as he and his movement were concerned, Stone stated, there was no reason they should not visibly unite since they were already one in spirit. Any reluctance to unite was on the part of the Reformers—the Campbell people—not from those on his side. He saw two reasons for their hesitance. First, the Stone Movement allowed unimmersed people to be members of their churches and to take communion. Stone churches taught that people were to believe, repent, and be immersed for the forgiveness of sins. But they could not make immersion as crucial to Christianity as the Campbell Movement had. They taught the truth about the importance and necessity of immersion, but exercised patience with those who were not convinced.

The second thing keeping them apart was the name each group had chosen. Like the Smith-Jones and O'Kelly churches, the Stone Movement had always simply used the name Christian. Campbell preferred the label Disciples, which Stone admitted was certainly a good scriptural name. But the Campbell churches used it, Stone asserted, to make sure no one confused them with the groups called Christian. It was a party name, just like Presbyterian or Baptist, because it distinguished those churches from other bodies of believers. Campbell responded with a sharp rebuke, claiming no one was asking them to give up the scriptural name Christian.

These articles and others that followed mirrored the deep differences between the two men and their movements. For example,

Barton Stone was opposed to traditional understandings of the Trinity. He did not see the doctrine taught in the New Testament as it appeared in most of the creeds and confessions, especially the Westminster Confession. Growing from his rejection of the Trinity was his view of Jesus. He was willing to accept every biblical statement about Christ at face value without question. But for him that meant accepting that Christ was not equal to the Father. He was Son of God and Savior; the Father exalted him to a place above all others and seated him at his right hand; but he was not equal to the Father. The equality of Father and Son simply didn't make sense to Stone.

Campbell, on the other hand, was quite traditional in his views of the godhead and the nature of Christ. While he agreed that the word "Trinity" was not in the Bible, he believed the sense of the community within God—one deity yet three persons—was essential to the Christian faith. To demote Christ from full divinity was to question the very center of Christian belief, that Jesus is able to save us!

Despite his strong rejection of Calvinist predestination, Stone held a rather pessimistic view of human nature. Humans were capable of understanding and responding appropriately to the gospel message. Yet he saw a wide role for the Holy Spirit as necessary in convicting and converting sinners. Furthermore, human society as a whole, he insisted, was on a downhill slide that only the Second Coming of Christ would stop.

Campbell saw things very differently. He was full of optimism about what humans could do by using their heads and working hard. America was the place prepared by God for the restoration of the church—the ancient gospel and order of things. After this restoration, all true Christians would come together, convert the world, and bring in the thousand-year reign of peace and prosperity on earth.

Stone and Campbell differed on their approach to evangelism. Stone had been a proponent of the revivals since his own experience at Cane Ridge. Here the Holy Spirit worked on the hearts of people to convict and convert them. Campbell hated the revivals and their raucous approach to conversion. Calm, clear, rational teaching of the gospel spelled out in the New Testament was the right way to convey truth and convince people to respond. The Holy Spirit worked through and along with the written word, never separately from it, to convince and convert sinners to Jesus.

Baptism was a point of difference as well. Campbell certainly believed there were those who enjoyed the benefits of Christ's pardon and salvation who had never been immersed because of innocent misunderstanding. He did teach, however, that in order to be part of the reform—to be a member in one of the churches in his movement—a person must be immersed because that was the clear teaching of Scripture. As mentioned already, while Stone and his followers taught immersion, they practiced "open membership," allowing non-immersed believers to be members of their congregations and to participate fully in the life of their churches.

The Stone churches celebrated the Lord's Supper infrequently while the Campbell churches celebrated it every week. The Stone churches had a much more developed sense of the need to organize the ministry. They distinguished between elders who were ordained ministers and those who were not officially ordained. The Campbell churches were extremely anti-clergy and much more democratic in their attitudes about who could do what in the church.

These were not minor differences! They reflected contradictory understandings of the nature of God, humankind, salvation, the church, and the end of time. How could two movements as dissimilar as these even consider uniting? It is hard to imagine, but thousands in both movements were convinced that the things they held in common far outweighed their differences. They agreed on the rejection of human creeds and confessions as tests of fellowship. They rejected loyalty to denominational bodies that separated them from other believers. All had a commitment to God and to his word as the only source of authority on religion. All wanted the unity of Christ's church.

There were some practical matters that made union a difficult undertaking. There were no central offices to make pronouncements about a union having taken place between the two groups. The only governing authority in either movement was each local congregation. There were no edicts from on high—the union had to happen in each city, town or village throughout the country. There had been stirrings of union as early as 1828 between a Stone congregation and a Campbell congregation in Bourbon County, Kentucky. A union did take place in Millersburg, Kentucky, in April 1831 and shortly afterward in Georgetown. However, meetings on December 31, 1831, and January 1, 1832, in Lexington, Kentucky, provided the real spark for the union movement.

The Union Takes Shape

Barton Stone, then living in Georgetown, had become fast friends with John T. Johnson (1788-1856), a former Baptist preacher who now followed Alexander Campbell's reform ideas. They had persuaded the two congregations in Georgetown to unite and proposed to hold four-day conferences at Georgetown on Christmas weekend and at the Hill Street church in Lexington on New Year's weekend to discuss the union efforts. Over two or three days several leaders from the two groups spoke, including one of the most widely known leaders of the Campbell Movement in Kentucky, Raccoon John Smith (1784-1868). Some of the speakers did not believe it was wise to try for a quick union between the two groups. They favored a gradual process that would allow them to grow together more naturally.

But the union occurred more quickly than some advised. Stone and Smith were the final speakers at the concluding session Saturday afternoon. Stone asked Smith to go first. Smith spoke of the fact that God has only one people on earth and that the Bible, the one book God had given Christians, exhorts them to be one family. He openly admitted that there were serious differences between the two movements, mentioning the issues of God's nature, the Trinity, and the atonement. These have been topics of discussion for centuries, he exclaimed, and are as far from settled now as they ever have been. The precise positions that Christians might take on these or any number of other issues are not part of the gospel. No heaven was promised to those who hold one position or the other, and no hell was threatened to those who deny them.

Only two things kept them from uniting immediately. Both groups should stop making deductions and inferences from Scripture into requirements for fellowship, but should simply use the words of Scripture when they spoke about these things. There should be more love for one another. Then Smith made one of the most famous statements in Stone-Campbell history. "Let us then, my brethren, be no longer Campbellites or Stoneites, New Lights or Old Lights, or any other kind of lights. But let us come to the Bible and the Bible alone, as the only book in creation that can give us all the Light we need."

Stone, after a brief statement, concluded that he had no objection to the basis of union Smith had laid down. He then turned and gave Smith his hand in fellowship, symbolizing the unity that was becoming a reality. The next day, a Sunday, the two congregations met together and took the Lord's Supper as one body. This service seemed to seal the union.

Stone was elated. In his report of the meeting in the *Christian Messenger*, he described the spirit of union as spreading like fire in dry stubble. He explained that the elders and people had commissioned John Smith and John Rogers (1800-1867), formerly of the Campbell and Stone Movements respectively, to travel among the churches to tell them what had happened in Lexington in order to "increase and consolidate the union." Smith and Rogers spent three years doing just that. Campbell took notice of the meeting in the March issue of his *Millennial Harbinger*, concluding that if the groups present

Raccoon John Smith Tombstone, Lexington, Ky

really had renounced their speculations, there was nothing to do but bid them Godspeed.

Further Roadblocks to Union

The road to unity was not easy. For many on both sides, the union seemed to mean giving up things they held dear. The old tensions over worship style were still there—the Stone churches being more emotionally expressive, the Campbell churches more rational and dignified. Notions about the work of the Holy Spirit and the name of the church continued to be problems for some. The Smith-Jones and O'Kelly Christian Churches that had been in fellowship with the Stone Movement were shocked at the union. They regarded Alexander Campbell as cold and rationalistic and suspected he had little or no real religion in him. They charged Stone with giving up the original vision of their reform.

A number of Stone congregations that chose not to participate in the union shared that sentiment. Most remained part of the loosely connected body of Christian Churches that included the churches of the Smith-Jones and O'Kelly Movements. As mentioned in chapter two, those churches merged in 1931 with the Congregational Church to form the Congregational Christian Church. Finally, that body merged in 1957 with the Evangelical and Reformed Church to form what today is the United Church of Christ.

When Stone moved to Jacksonville, Illinois, in 1834, he found that the two congregations in the town, one from his movement and one from the Campbell Movement, still worshipped separately. He refused to worship with either until they united. An even more startling incident shows just how difficult the union process really was. The month after the wonderful unity communion service on January 1, 1832, in Lexington, the two groups experienced what one reporter described as a "blow up." The Stone people insisted that there had to be an ordained minister (elder) present to administer the Lord's Supper. Since no elder was there, and the Campbell people thought such a requirement was ridiculous, the two groups in Lexington decided that they could not unite for the time being. It would be three more years before the two congregations would actually become one for good.

The proper name for this united movement challenges historians. As we saw above, some used "Disciples" or "Disciples of Christ" to describe both individuals in the movement and the united church as a whole. Others preferred "Christian Churches" or "Churches of Christ" to describe the movement or specific congregations. In order to avoid confusion with the current Christian Church (Disciples of Christ) or with current Churches of Christ, we will use the term Stone-Campbell Movement for the united church from 1832 until 1906.

Real Unity

Even with all the problems involved, the story of the union of the Stone and Campbell Movements is phenomenal. How was it possible for two groups that were as different from each other as today's Christian Churches and Churches of Christ and Assemblies of God to even consider coming together? It happened because the people involved believed union was God's will and that they shared what was most important in Christianity—one body, one Spirit, one Lord, one faith, one baptism, one God and Father of all. Most of all, they loved one another as fellow children of God with all their imperfections.

Christian unity may not always mean a physical merger of congregations or movements. But when Christians are convinced of the importance of unity and are willing to put up with each others' peculiarities in the knowledge that all are committed to knowing and doing God's will expressed in scripture, the kind of unity seen in this chapter from our history may be the best and fullest kind there is.

Questions for Discussion

1. How did the personalities of Stone and Campbell help or hurt the union?

2. How important is it for local congregations to agree internally on most doctrinal issues?

3. Should basic doctrinal agreement with the leaders and other members of a congregation be a requirement for membership?

4. What do you think was the most serious doctrinal difference between the Stone and Campbell Movements at the time of the union? Why do you believe that one is the most serious?

5. Would the doctrinal difference(s) you chose in question four prevent you from approving a union with a group that held a view other than your own?

6. Would it be possible today for local congregations to experience a union like those that occurred in the 1830s and following? If so, how? If not, why?

7. Are there any ways that Christian Churches and Churches of Christ can act together as a whole?

For Further Reading

Garrett, Leroy. *The Stone-Campbell Movement: The Story of the American Restoration Movement*. Joplin, Missouri: College Press, 1994. See pages 174-196.

McAllister, Lester G., and William E. Tucker. *Journey in Faith: A History of the Christian Church (Disciples of Christ)*. St. Louis: The Bethany Press, 1975. See pages 146-155.

Murch, James DeForest. *Christians Only: A History of the Restoration Movement*. Cincinnati, Standard Publishing, 1962. See pages 109-121.

North, James B. Union in Truth: *An Interpretive History of the Restoration Movement*. Cincinnati: Standard Publishing, 1994. See pages 155-185.

Williams, John Augustus. *Life of Elder John Smith: With Some Account of the Rise and Progress of the Current Reformation*. Cincinnati: R. W. Carroll, 1871. See chapter 9, pages 367-378.

The Growth of the Stone-Campbell Movement

When the Stone and Campbell Movements began to unite in 1832, they together numbered around 25,000 members, mainly in Kentucky and Ohio. By 1861, the united movement numbered almost 200,000 in twenty-nine states and two territories. It was during this period that the Disciples of Christ (as they were generally known) became a nationwide church, by some estimates the fourth largest religious group in the country.

Walter Scott and the New Evangelism

This phenomenal growth largely resulted from the influence of one man, Walter Scott (1796-1861). Born in Scotland, Scott grew up in the Church of Scotland and received his education at the University of Edinburgh. In 1818, he came to America, eventually settling near Pittsburgh. There he taught school and worshiped with a Scottish Baptist church.

In 1821, Scott met Alexander Campbell, and they soon became friends. Scott contributed articles on evangelism to the initial issue

Walter Scott

of Campbell's *Christian Baptist* (Scott was the one who suggested the name for the journal). Campbell thought so highly of Scott that he nominated him for appointment as a traveling evangelist for the Mahoning Baptist Association.

In 1827, the Mahoning Association did appoint Scott as their evangelist. The year before, the seventeen churches in the Association had a total of thirty-four baptisms. In his first year as evangelist, Scott had nearly a thousand baptisms, doubling the size of most of the churches. Indeed, Scott averaged a thousand baptisms per year for the next thirty years of his life.

What made him so successful was a new method of evangelism. Although the churches of the Campbell Movement had been in existence for several years and all practiced believer's immersion, they had not found a simple answer to the question, "What must I do to be saved?" In his study of Scripture, Scott found that answer which he called "the ancient gospel" or (in the words of one of his later book titles) *The Gospel Restored.*

Scott originally summarized that gospel under six points. Humans should do three things to be saved: believe, repent, and be baptized. God makes three promises to those who do these things: forgiveness of sins, the gift of the Holy Spirit, and eternal life. Eventually, Scott reduced the six to an easily remembered "five-finger exercise"—faith, repentance, baptism, forgiveness of sins, and the gift of the Holy Spirit.

Such a formula could become legalistic. What kept Scott from using it in a legalistic way was his constant emphasis on the central teaching of Christianity, that Jesus is the Christ. Scott called this "the golden oracle," later writing a massive volume entitled *The Messiahship, or Great Demonstration, Written for the Union of Christians, on Christian Principles, as Plead for in the Current Reformation*. This lengthy title shows that Scott's view of restoration was directly in line with that of Stone and the Campbells. Restoration centered on Christ for the purpose of uniting all Christians.

Why was Scott's "five-finger" approach so successful? Because many on the frontier were under the influence of a strict Calvinism that said one could do nothing to be saved, since salvation depended solely on the work of God's predestination. Many went to Calvinistic revivals and sat on the mourner's or anxious bench, trying to "pray through" until God sent a sign of their election. Many never received such a sign and felt they were destined for destruction.

By contrast, Scott told these independent frontier people that there was something they could do to be saved. Salvation was for all who would believe, repent, and be baptized. Many received this message with great relief and joy, rushing forward to confess their faith and be baptized.

Although Scott began his preaching of the restored gospel before the union with the Stone Movement in 1832, evangelists in the united Movement copied his method, accounting for much of the growth of the Disciples through the nineteenth century. This is why many consider him one of the four founders of the movement along with Barton Stone, Thomas Campbell, and Alexander Campbell.

Schools and Colleges

Many of the early leaders, including Thomas and Alexander Campbell, saw themselves foremost as teachers. It is not surprising, then, that the Stone-Campbell Movement, along with every major religious group in nineteenth century America, began colleges and schools. Unlike many other religious schools of the period, training ministers was not the primary purpose of the Disciple colleges. Instead, they focused on broad training in the arts and sciences using the empirical method popularized in seventeenth century England and Scotland.

Bethany College

The first college in the movement was Bacon College, Georgetown, Kentucky, founded in 1836 primarily as an engineering school. Walter Scott served briefly as its first President. Named after Sir Francis Bacon (1561-1626), the school emphasized his experimental method in the sciences and even in moral teaching. In

1839, Bacon College moved to Harrodsburg, Kentucky, was rechartered in 1858 as Kentucky University, and later merged with other schools to become Transylvania University in Lexington.

In 1841, Alexander Campbell founded Bethany College near his home in Bethany, West Virginia. Bethany also depended heavily on the empirical method, with more than half of the curriculum in the sciences. Bethany's charter prohibited the establishment of a theological professorship. At the same time, Campbell could boast that Bethany was the only college founded on the Bible, in that students heard a one-hour Bible lecture each day. This reflects the movement's insistence on objective, empirical Bible study, as opposed to what some called disdainfully, "speculative theology." Bethany College is still in its original location and still associated with Disciples of Christ.

Franklin College near Nashville, Tennessee, began in 1845. Tolbert Fanning (1810-1874), the founder of the school, did not believe in endowments for colleges. That partially explains the short life of Franklin College. Closed by the Civil War in 1861, it reopened briefly in 1865, but soon closed permanently as the result of a campus fire.

For a while, these were the three major colleges in the movement, although numerous schools and colleges sprang up wherever it spread. From 1840-1866, Disciples began thirty-two colleges including (with their founding dates) Burritt College, Spencer, Tennessee (1848); Hiram College, Hiram, Ohio (1850); Butler University, Indianapolis, Indiana (1854); Culver-Stockton College, Canton, Missouri (1853); and Eureka College, Eureka, Illinois (1855).

Although not intended primarily for ministerial training, the colleges served that function. Many of the significant leaders in the church in the nineteenth century were products of the colleges, particularly Bethany. In a congregationally organized movement, the colleges provided one means of fellowship and unity of thought among the churches.

Papers, Publications, and Debates

Religious papers also provided unity (and sometimes disunity) to the movement, serving as the forum to discuss ideas and issues.

An old truism is that the Disciples did not have bishops but had editors who sometimes ruled with an iron fist.

Alexander Campbell's influence grew primarily through his monthly periodicals, first the *Christian Baptist* (1823-1830), then the *Millennial Harbinger* (1830-1866). There is a marked difference in tone between the two journals reflecting Campbell's changed circumstances. He filled the *Christian Baptist* with sarcastic denunciations of the religious follies of the age. The *Harbinger* was intentionally more positive in tone, befitting Campbell's position as the leader of a large movement among Protestants.

Other leaders greatly extended their influence through journals. Barton Stone edited the *Christian Messenger* from 1826-1844. Walter Scott had the aptly named *Evangelist* (1832-1844). In 1855, Tolbert Fanning (1810-1874) founded the influential *Gospel Advocate*. The *American Christian Review*, edited from 1858 by Benjamin Franklin (1812-1878), eventually became the most widely read paper in the movement.

In addition, there were dozens of short-lived papers with limited circulation (including one named the *Heretic Detector*). These papers did indeed detect heresy, debate issues, promote unity, and suggest programs. More than any other factor, the journals formed the web that held the Stone-Campbell Movement together.

Other printed material besides periodicals helped shape our thought, especially the published works of Alexander Campbell. Campbell published one of the first modern translations of the New Testament (usually known as the *Living Oracles*) in 1826. The translation never became popular even among the Disciples. More influential was his *Christian System* (1836), the earliest systematic theology of the movement (although Campbell would be horrified by that term).

Religious debates were a common way of disseminating ideas in the nineteenth century. Campbell and his opponents were always gentlemanly in debate and drew large crowds. The debates reached a wide audience in their published form. His debate with Robert Owen (1771-1858), the Welsh skeptic and social reformer, made Campbell a household name. In the debate, held in Cincinnati in 1829, Campbell's eloquent presentation of the traditional

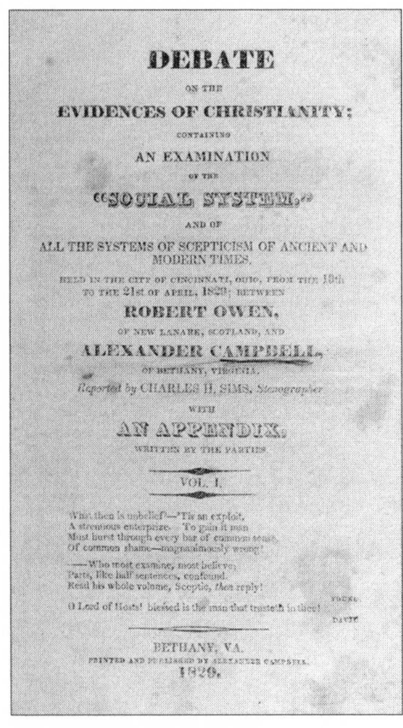

DEBATE

ON THE

EVIDENCES OF CHRISTIANITY;

CONTAINING

AN EXAMINATION

OF THE

"SOCIAL SYSTEM,"

AND OF

ALL THE SYSTEMS OF SCEPTICISM OF ANCIENT AND MODERN TIMES.

HELD IN THE CITY OF CINCINNATI, OHIO, FROM THE 13th TO THE 21st OF APRIL, 1829; BETWEEN

ROBERT OWEN,

OF NEW LANARK, SCOTLAND, AND

ALEXANDER CAMPBELL,

OF BETHANY, VIRGINIA.

Reported by CHARLES H. SIMS, *Stenographer*

WITH

AN APPENDIX,

WRITTEN BY THE PARTIES.

VOL. I.

What then is unbelief?—'Tis an exploit,
A strenuous enterprize. To gain it man
Must burst through every bar of common sense,
Of common shame—magnanimously wrong!

——Who most examine, most believe.
Parts, like half sentences, confound.
Read his whole volume, Sceptic, *then* reply! YOUNG.

O Lord of Hosts! blessed is the man that trusteth in thee! DAVID.

BETHANY, VA.

PRINTED AND PUBLISHED BY ALEXANDER CAMPBELL.

1829.

Campbell-Owen Debate

arguments for the existence of God established his reputation as the American champion of the Christian faith, standing against the destructive force of European free thought.

In 1837, also in Cincinnati, Campbell debated Bishop John B. Purcell of the Roman Catholic Church. The discussion mainly dealt with issues surrounding public education. Campbell defended the Protestant character of public schooling against Purcell's promotion of parochial schools. Thus, in this debate Campbell was the spokesman for Protestantism, not just for the Disciples.

Campbell's longest published debate was in 1843 in Lexington, Kentucky, with Presbyterian minister N.L. Rice. It dealt with issues more specific to the cause of the movement, like believer's immersion versus infant baptism.

Of course, Alexander Campbell was not the only leader to have debates or publish papers and books. But his publishing greatly increased his influence. Through his monthly periodicals, occasional pamphlets, a Bible translation, hymnbooks, published debates, and other books, he proclaimed the basic principles, set the boundaries, and dealt with specific issues for the movement. It was the press above all that allowed him to give form and direction to a church, the Disciples or Christians, that had no central organization, but was organized congregationally.

Becoming Organized for Missions

That congregational organization posed a difficulty for international mission work, since few single congregations could support a missionary. In the early days of the *Christian Baptist*, Alexander

Campbell had written against missionary societies, claiming the early church worked only in its local capacity.

By the 1840's, Campbell had changed his mind. He now led a large movement influential in the larger culture, and Campbell felt they would not reach their full potential for service without a cooperative organization among the congregations. From 1845-1848, he penned a series of articles in the *Millennial Harbinger* on church cooperation, eventually calling for a church-wide organization to promote missions.

As early as 1829, church leaders in local areas had met to share information and encouragement. By 1844, regular statewide meetings had occurred in Kentucky, Ohio, Indiana, and Tennessee. The first organizations formed in response to the call for church-wide support among the Disciples were the American Christian Bible Society, begun in 1845, and the Sunday School and Tract Society, begun in 1846. David S. Burnet (1808-1867) led both organizations and also took the initiative in beginning the Missionary Society.

Campbell had called for a general convention of the Disciples in Cincinnati in November 1849. The hope was for each congregation to send delegates to the convention, but many congregations did not participate and several individuals simply came on their own. The convention was therefore more of a mass meeting of 151 "messengers" from about 100 churches than a representative body. Out of this meeting came the American Christian Missionary Society, with Alexander Campbell chosen as its first President (although Campbell himself was not present due to illness).

As we will see in chapter nine, the right of the Missionary Society to exist eventually became a divisive issue among Disciples, contributing to the split between Disciples of Christ and Churches of Christ. What concerns us here is the Society's role in sending the first Disciple missionaries from America to other countries.

Since Jerusalem was where Peter first preached the gospel in the Book of Acts, it seemed fitting that the first missionary supported by the Society should take the restored gospel there. They chose James T. Barclay (1807-1874), a well-educated physician, for the task. Barclay and his family had two tours of duty in

Jerusalem, 1850-1854 and 1858-1861. They went knowing nothing of the languages spoken there and little of the culture. They made a few converts, but left no lasting church.

Barclay received criticism from many in the Society for being a slave owner. The general disapproval of slavery among the Disciples led the Society to buy the freedom of a Kentucky-born slave, Alexander Cross, and send him as a missionary to freed slaves in Liberia. Cross left for Liberia in 1854, but died of fever two months after his arrival.

The only early mission that had even modest success was that of the third Society missionary, J.O. Beardslee (1814-1879), who worked in Jamaica from 1858-1866. But false allegations even clouded his work.

Since these were the only missionaries sent by the Society before the Civil War, one is tempted to call its efforts a failure. Yet, what may be most significant about the Society is not what it accomplished in missions but what it said about the developing identity of the Disciples. From two small fellowships in 1832, the church had grown through evangelism, education, and publications to be a formidable religious body, capable of organizing for international action.

Questions for Discussion

1. What was Walter Scott's greatest contribution to the Stone-Campbell Movement?

2. What were the six points Scott used to summarize the gospel? Is this a fair summary? What did he omit or what should he have omitted?

3. List some of the early colleges founded by members of the Stone-Campbell Movement. What were these colleges like? How did they affect the churches?

4. List some of the religious papers in the early movement. How did these affect the churches?

5. Who were the first three international missionaries of the movement? Where were they sent? How were they supported? What does this say about the movement in the late 1800's?

For Further Reading

Garrett, Leroy. *The Stone-Campbell Movement*. Joplin, Missouri: College Press, 1994. See Pages 143-172.

McAllister, Lester G. and Tucker, William E. *Journey in Faith*. Saint Louis: Chalice Press, 1975. See Pages 129-188.

Toulouse, Mark G., ed. *Walter Scott: A Nineteenth Century Evangelical*. Saint Louis: Chalice Press, 1999.

Webb, Henry E. *In Search of Christian Unity: A History of the Restoration Movement*, revised edition. Abilene, TX: ACU Press, 2003. See Pages 127-192.

West, Earl Irvin. *The Search for the Ancient Order*, Vol. 1. Nashville: Gospel Advocate, 1986. See pages 76-126.

Developing a Theology

"Theology" was a bad word for early leaders of the Movement. Barton Stone, Alexander Campbell, and all the other early Restoration leaders condemned the term. To them "theology" smelled like divisive speculation. Theology, particularly as expressed in the detailed creeds of their day, divided Christians. They wanted Christ to unite them. This early objection to the term "theology" persists today. Some colleges still have courses in "Christian Doctrine" but not in "Systematic Theology."

But if we define theology as "thoughtful reflection on the Christian faith," then it is clear that all Christians have a theology. Campbell and others were right to point out that it is faith in Christ, not theology, which saves. These early leaders, however, did have a thoughtful faith. They had a particular approach to Christianity, shaped by their time and experience. So do we. So do all Christians. We all have a theology. The question is, will it be a well-thought-out theology, or will we thoughtlessly accept what others tell us about the faith? It was this mindless acceptance of traditionalism that the early Restoration leaders opposed.

In a brief space, we cannot fully discuss the complete theology of every early Restoration leader. Instead, we will focus on three aspects of the thought of Alexander Campbell that still influence his heirs: his view of Restoration and unity, his approach to understanding the Bible, and his view of baptism and what it means to be a Christian.

Unity and Restoration

At the heart of our early theology is the desire to restore to the church important elements it had lost through the ages, especially its unity. As we saw in chapter four, when Thomas Campbell penned the *Declaration and Address* in 1809, his primary theme was the unity of the church: "Prop. 1. That the Church of Christ upon earth is essentially, intentionally, and constitutionally one." Thomas Campbell believed the church could enjoy that unity if it would leave behind the doctrines that divided Christians to practice those teachings "expressly exhibited" in the New Testament. That phrase and others such as "plain," "clear," "manifest," "simple" and "original pattern" occur more than sixty times in the *Declaration and Address*. To Thomas Campbell, the essentials of the faith and the shape of the church should be plain to all.

However, he never spelled out exactly what the express shape of the church was and should be. His son, Alexander Campbell, was not so reticent. In a series of thirty articles on "A Restoration of the Ancient Order of Things," published in the *Christian Baptist* between 1825 and 1829, Alexander attempted to lay out the original pattern of the church as he saw it.

The content of most of Campbell's articles is not surprising to those of us in Christian Churches and Churches of Christ. Five of the articles deal with general principles of restoration. Two list the dangers of creeds. Nine of the thirty articles are on worship, with four arguing for weekly communion. Five articles are on church offices: bishop, deacon, and others.

What might surprise some who unfairly characterize Campbell as an unfeeling rationalist are the two articles on the "Spirit and Temper of Mind of the Ancient Order," and "Devotion to God's Will" in which Campbell recounts his own religious experience. Also surprising to contemporary church members are his seven articles on "Church Discipline." To Campbell, the purpose of restoring the ancient order was not to be legalistically correct, but to make the church the school of discipleship and devotion to Christ that it was intended to be.

Why did the Campbells speak so much about the church to the neglect of other doctrines? Did they think the doctrines about God, Christ, the Holy Spirit, salvation, and last things were less important than the church? No. Both Campbells had a broad theological and classical education and could place the doctrine of the church in a broader theological context. So why didn't they teach more about those foundational doctrines instead of focusing on the church?

The Campbells could assume most of those foundational doctrines because they believed most Protestant teaching in their day was correct. They wanted to remove unwanted additions to the church and restore to it aspects that had been lost through the years. Their purpose was "...to bring the Christianity and the church of the present up to the New Testament standard." In attempting to do so, they found that much of the Christianity of their day was sound and original. They generally agreed with Protestants on their view of God and Christ, and even on salvation (except on believer's immersion for remission of sins). One area where they felt Protestantism was deficient was in certain aspects of its doctrine of the church. That is what needed restoring.

Alexander Campbell's treatment of the Apostles' Creed clearly shows his approach. Although he consistently opposed creeds as tests of fellowship, he nevertheless says, "We never objected to a creed properly so called. We have a creed—an apostolic creed." He then goes on to quote the Apostles' Creed and adds to it baptism for remission of sins, weekly communion, and other "facts or articles of belief." Campbell did not emphasize the basic articles of the Apostles' Creed, even though he thought them central in importance, because the churches of his day already believed them. Instead, he focused on those areas the church still lacked. In restoring an old house, one can ignore the foundation if it is sound. That does not make it less important but less needful of urgent attention.

This explains why theology in Christian Churches and Churches of Christ is not so much thin as uneven and spotty. We have overemphasized some doctrines at the expense of others that were as important, if not more important. The doctrine of the church is one area where our theology has been strong, so strong in fact, that it has tended to eclipse all other doctrines.

This early view of restoration has other implications. It implies that restoration is an on-going process. The church will be restored and ever restoring until the coming of Christ. As we will see, later some in the movement felt we had completely restored the church and only needed to defend and preserve it. This was not the original restoration plea.

The early idea of restoration was also not an end in itself. Restoration was for the purpose of unity. Later some felt that one must choose between restoration and unity. Our early leaders felt they should always go together.

Interpreting the Bible

Alexander Campbell gives his method of Bible interpretation in his book, *The Christian System*. His rules reflect common sense and the best biblical scholarship of his time. His approach had its roots in the Enlightenment enterprise that sought to free the Bible from sectarian strife by reading it scientifically, that is, grammatically and historically, as one would read any other book. He thus bequeathed to his followers a strong historical approach to Scripture. But he is not a thoroughgoing Enlightenment rationalist. Indeed, his most important, "indispensable" rule is: "We must come within the understanding distance." One may follow all the rules of reason and still not hear God in Scripture. To understand truly, one must be "ravished with the moral scenes that the Bible unfolds." One must have "one ardent desire—intent only to know the will of God."

Campbell regarded the heart as the seat of our deepest moral intentions, giving it preeminence over reason. We must read the Bible with more than the mind. True, Campbell sometimes spoke as if he equates heart with mind, but a close reading of his work shows he transcended the strict rationalism of his day by giving precedence to obedience from the heart over understanding with the mind. He called for pious scholars who put the word into practice.

Campbell's hermeneutic (his method of Bible interpretation) was also Christocentric. He taught that one should use the best contemporary methods of Bible interpretation, but must always keep the focus on heart-felt relationship to Christ. This prevents his hermeneutic from becoming fixed and legalistic. Later, some parts of the movement developed a more narrow hermeneutic focusing on what practices the Bible authorizes. While the early restoration leaders certainly felt strongly that rightly handling the scriptures and arriving at correct teaching was important, they all stressed the Bible's portrait of Christ more than a specific interpretive strategy.

Baptism and Sectarianism

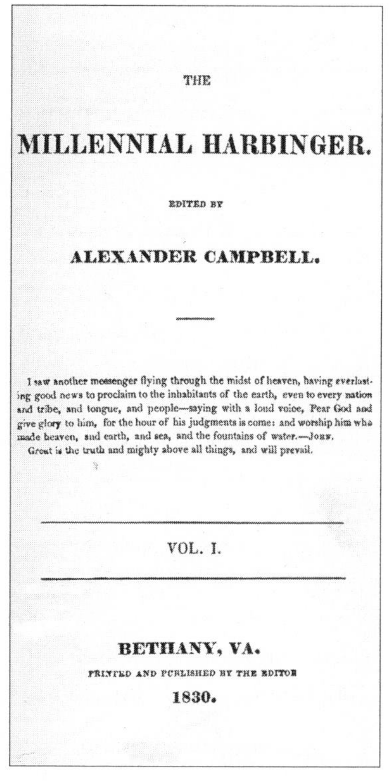
THE

MILLENNIAL HARBINGER.

EDITED BY

ALEXANDER CAMPBELL.

I saw another messenger flying through the midst of heaven, having everlasting good news to proclaim to the inhabitants of the earth, even to every nation and tribe, and tongue, and people—saying with a loud voice, Fear God and give glory to him, for the hour of his judgments is come: and worship him who made heaven, and earth, and sea, and the fountains of water.—John.

Great is the truth and mighty above all things, and will prevail.

VOL. I.

BETHANY, VA.

PRINTED AND PUBLISHED BY THE EDITOR

1830.

More than any other teaching, the early leaders' insistence on believer's immersion for forgiveness of sins set them apart from other Christian groups. Even Baptists, who practiced believer's immersion, did not emphasize its role in salvation as strongly as our movement did.

Early in the history of the movement, some wondered if this emphasis on baptism would become divisive and sectarian. In 1830 Barton Stone worried that insisting on immersion could become a one-item sectarian creed that would exclude more Christians from union than any creed in existence. With some in the movement, this fear would become a reality. They would exclude all the unimmersed from the very name, "Christian."

In 1837, an unnamed woman from Lunenburg, Virginia, wrote Alexander Campbell expressing her surprise at his statement that he found Christians in all the Protestant groups. Campbell printed the letter in the *Millennial Harbinger* because it allowed him to answer several questions: Are only immersed believers entitled to the name Christian? Are all the Christians in the world in the movement Campbell led? Can we call the unimmersed "Christians" and still insist they be immersed?

Campbell was adamant in his reply to the letter: there must be Christians among the Protestant sects. Otherwise, he argued, there would have been no Christians in the world for centuries and Jesus' promise that the gates of hell would not prevail against the church (Matthew 16:18) would have proved false. Campbell said, "This cannot be; and therefore there are Christians among the sects."

The plea for unity, to "come out" of sectarianism, itself implies that there are Christians in the denominations. If all the Christians in the world were already united in the Stone-Campbell churches, then why would Campbell and others call Christians to come out of their sectarianism? In other words, to plead for unity necessarily means there are Christians to unify. Unfortunately, there were some even in Campbell's day who thought he wished to "make and lead a large exclusivist party" who claimed to be the only ones who were saved. He vehemently denied this, saying, "I think there are many, in most Protestant parties, whose errors and mistakes I hope the Lord will forgive."

Thus those in his day and our own who think they are the only Christians are out of step with the ideas that shaped us in the beginning. Some have tried to paint Alexander Campbell as inconsistent on this issue, claiming the "early Campbell" was a strict restorationist who saw his followers (or perhaps all the immersed) as the only Christians, while the "later Campbell" abandoned that position and became more ecumenical. Campbell himself refutes this charge by quoting his writings from the early years to show that he had always believed there are Christians among the sects.

The belief that there are Christians among the sects raises the question of baptism. As the Lunenburg letter asks, "What act of yours gave you the name of Christian?" In his preaching, his writing, and his debates, Campbell had strongly defended believers immersion as the biblical form of baptism and had called on those baptized as infants to be immersed as adults. This emphasis led some of his followers to assume that only the immersed were Christians. They were shocked to find Campbell calling at least some of the unimmersed "Christians," and they accused him of abandoning his position on the importance of biblical baptism.

He replied by accusing some of his correspondents of being "ultraists," that is, legalists, on the subject of baptism. They had made baptism itself a savior, claiming it was the single standard by which one is judged to be a Christian. Campbell never taught such "water salvation." He refused to make even immersion the single standard of Christian faith and character. If forced to choose between one baptized as an infant and one immersed as a believer, he preferred the one who loved Christ most, saying, "Did I act otherwise, I would be a pure sectarian, a Pharisee among Christians."

Although baptism is important, Campbell wrote, it is not more important than Christian character. To deny the name Christian to those who display the character of Christ is to be the worst kind of sectarian. It is to promote the legalistic, exclusivist barriers that Campbell worked all his life to tear down.

So, if the unimmersed are Christians, does that mean immersion is not essential for salvation and is relatively unimportant? No, Campbell says, baptism is still "unto salvation." How then can the unimmersed be saved? Campbell's answer is that some of the unimmersed who were baptized as infants have never thought to inquire whether their baptism was scriptural, but took such for granted. Paul talks of one who does not have outward circumcision, but has inward circumcision. In the same way, Campbell asks, "Can a person who simply, not perversely, mistakes the outer baptism, have the inward?"

Campbell strongly denied that admitting there may be Christians among the sects detracts from the importance of baptism. He saw himself steering a middle course between essentialists and nonessentialists on baptism. He claimed he did not detract from the authority of baptism simply by admitting the bare possibility of one being saved without it.

So, if Campbell believed immersion was not absolutely essential to salvation, did he advocate open membership in the church? No. He would not call everyone "brother" who called God "Father."

Obedience to Christ and his ordinances (including baptism) were usual conditions essential to salvation. In this, Campbell claims to agree with all Christians, Catholic and Protestant, who believe one who willfully disdains or neglects baptism cannot be saved.

But one can obey only to the extent of his or her knowledge. If one does not know baptism is believer's immersion, then one cannot obey. However, one who knows and rejects the ordinance is without excuse. Campbell told all who would listen to him that scriptural baptism was immersion for forgiveness of sins. Such was required to be recognized as a member of his congregation. He did not downplay baptism to increase numbers. Neither did he judge all the unimmersed to be outside of Christ.

Theology Then and Now

In many ways, what still makes Christian Churches and Churches of Christ distinctive comes from the theology of Campbell on these subjects. We want to restore what the church has lost for the sake of uniting Christians. We are a back to the Bible movement that uses the best of contemporary scholarship to understand Scripture, but we always want to see Christ in our Bible study. We insist on baptism as an essential expression of saving faith, but we do not claim to be the only Christians. In these and other areas, a twenty-first century church can still learn from the ideals of the nineteenth-century Disciples.

Questions for Discussion

1. Is "theology" a good word or a bad word to you? Is it best to avoid the term or is it helpful if properly defined?

2. Why did the Campbells teach so much on the church to the neglect of other doctrines? Should we have the same emphasis on the church or have times changed?

3. What was Alexander Campbell's approach to hermeneutics (understanding the Bible)? Does this approach work today? What are its strengths and weaknesses?

4. What did the early Restoration leaders mean when they said, "Christians only, not the only Christians?" Does accepting others as Christians mean we must abandon our emphasis on believers' immersion for forgiveness of sins?

For Further Reading

For the text of Alexander Campbell's discussion of the Lunenburg Letter, see http://www.bible.acu.edu/stone-campbell/Etexts/lun16.html

Boring, M. Eugene. *Disciples and the Bible*. St Louis: Chalice Press, 1997.

Hicks, John Mark, "Alexander Campbell on Christians Among the Sects," in David W. Fletcher, ed. *Baptism and the Remission of Sins*. Joplin, Missouri: College Press, 1990. See pages 171-202.

Hicks, John Mark and Bobby Valentine. *Down in the River to Pray: Revisioning Baptism as God's Transforming Work*. Abilene, Texas: Leafwood Publishers, 2004. See pages 131-151.

Lawrence, Kenneth, ed. *Classic Themes of Disciple Theology*. Fort Worth: Texas Christian University Press, 1986.

Richesin, L. Dale and Bouchard, Larry D., eds. *Interpreting Disciples: Practical Theology in the Disciples of Christ*. Fort Worth: Texas Christian University Press, 1987.

Sprinkle, Stephen V. *Disciples and Theology*. St. Louis: Chalice Press, 1999.

The Great Divide of the Civil War

Until recently, almost every history of the Stone-Campbell Movement explicitly denied that the Civil War divided us. Other bodies like the Methodists, Baptists, and Presbyterians suffered division into northern and southern groups, but not us. Moses Lard (1818-1880), a prominent Missouri preacher and editor, made the classic statement on this. Like most of the first generation leaders, Lard had urged members of the churches to refuse to fight in the war. Christians should avoid entanglement in such divisive political matters. In 1866, Lard admitted in his quarterly journal that the war had "cooled many an ardent feeling and caused old friends to regard one another a little shyly." Yet in the end, he insisted, the war had caused no division in our ranks.

Lard's remarks have more to do with his notions of unity and division among Christians than they do with the Civil War. Still, his declaration that we had not divided carried the day for generations. We need to reexamine that statement, however, because the sectional feelings burned into the American mind by the events surrounding that terrible war shaped us as much as they did all other Americans.

Slavery and the Churches

In 1860, there were about 1200 congregations in the north and about 800 in the south. Many were in border states like Kentucky, Ohio and Missouri where differences over the issues that led to war were especially strong. Though many difficult

Moses Lard

political and social issues fueled the conflict, at its very heart it was about slavery and race. Members of the churches of the Stone-Campbell Movement were just as much a part of the heated discussions as anyone. Their attitudes about blacks and slavery reflected the same spectrum as the rest of America.

Both Barton W. Stone and Alexander Campbell opposed slavery but were just as opposed to abolitionism—the immediate freeing of all slaves by law. Both men owned slaves at different times in their lives. Stone freed all his slaves by 1804, but later the law prevented him from emancipating several others he inherited from his wife's mother. He was a supporter of the American Colonization Society for several years. This group planned to end slavery over time by buying slaves from masters and sending them "back" to the west African nation of Liberia, purchased and established by the society for that purpose.

Campbell detailed his position on slavery in 1845 in a series of eight articles published in the *Millennial Harbinger* entitled "Our Position to American Slavery." The Methodist and Baptist Churches had just divided over slavery, and the debate over the annexation of Texas to the Union as a slave state threatened a major crisis in the nation and the movement.

He spent much energy explaining why the issue of slavery must not divide the churches. Though opposed to the institution, he appeared to be defending its existence in most of the articles! Nowhere in the Scriptures, he claimed, is the relation of master to slave sinful and immoral in itself. On the contrary, the Scriptures seek to regulate the relationship, not abolish it. When he finally began to explain why he opposed slavery, it was, in his words, a matter of expediency. Sounding much like his fellow Virginian Thomas Jefferson, Campbell insisted that in the civilized world slavery was simply not in harmony with the spirit of the age or the advancement of society. It was a hindrance to personal and national prosperity and imposed so many burdens on Christian slave owners that it worked against the kind of domestic happiness everyone really wanted. He described a gradual approach as the best way to end slavery without causing disruption to the nation and its institutions.

Campbell was not primarily interested in the welfare of the slaves. He was interested in the unity of his reform movement and regarded the conflict over slavery as a potential threat. He concluded his series with the assertion that "no Christian community, governed by the Bible, can constitutionally and rightfully make the simple relation of master and slave a term of Christian fellowship or a subject of discipline."

Campbell's attempt to state a "moderate" position that would defuse tension over the issue only seemed to make people on both sides mad at him. John Kirk, a church leader in Ohio, wrote Campbell in 1851 that slave-holders who had crept into the church, after being admonished to free their slaves, if they refused, "should be dealt with as we would with a horse thief or any other notorious villain." Kirk said that most of the members of the churches in his part of Ohio disagreed with Campbell on the subject of slavery. He ended his subscription to the *Millennial Harbinger* and stated he would not patronize any paper whose editor would not denounce the Fugitive Slave law and the government that passed it.

Pardee Butler (1816-1888) was perhaps the most outspoken abolitionist in the Stone-Campbell Movement. When he moved to Kansas in 1855 to work as an evangelist, his message was as much abolitionism as gospel. When the American Christian Missionary Society insisted that Butler stop preaching his anti-slavery views, a group of abolitionist church members from Ohio and Indiana formed a rival missionary society in 1859 that provided funds for Butler's work until it was dissolved in 1863.

Without question, the strongest pro-slavery voice in the Stone-Campbell Movement was James Shannon (1799-1859). He asserted what many whites took for granted, that blacks were inferior and not capable of living responsibly as free people. Nature, the United States Constitution, and the Bible all clearly approved slavery, he said, and any attempt to violate the rights of masters to hold slaves as legal property should be resisted even to the point of war.

Butler and Shannon represented the opposite ends of the spectrum on the issue. Many church members were content to take Campbell's position and stay out of the fights. However, that became almost impossible with the outbreak of the war in 1861. Opinions were most diverse and tensions greatest in the "border" states like Kentucky and Missouri. Just as with later divisive issues like instrumental music and missionary societies, the question of slavery and slaveholders was a matter each congregation had to work out for itself. We didn't have a national organization that could facilitate the kind of division seen among the Baptists, Methodists, and Presbyterians. Or did we?

The Churches in the Civil War

Though by no means working like a Presbyterian General Assembly or Methodist Conference, the Stone-Campbell Movement did have a national organization—the American Christian Missionary Society. Headquartered in the north, in Cincinnati, Ohio, the annual meetings had always enjoyed attendance from across the country. When the war began, Southerners were no longer able to come to meetings.

Just as many leaders in the movement had been "moderates" on the issue of slavery, many (led again by Campbell himself) refused to endorse either side in the war. It is not surprising, then, that outsiders began to question the loyalty to the Union of the missionary society and the churches it represented. At the October 1861 meeting, some members introduced a resolution calling on the churches of the movement to do everything in their power to support the Union. The society itself did not adopt this resolution, since some insisted that political resolutions like this one were outside the legitimate business of the missionary society. So they called a ten-minute recess, voted on it as a mass meeting rather than as the society, and approved the resolution.

Technically, the American Christian Missionary Society did not pass the resolution. No matter. When word got back to southern church leaders the reaction was swift. Tolbert Fanning in Nashville, Tennessee, had been urging southern Christians to stay out of the conflict. When he heard about the resolution, he took it to mean that the ACMS was encouraging its supporters to join the Union armies and participate in the murder of the southern people. Unless those who had passed this resolution repented of what they had done, Fanning was clear that he could not regard them as brothers.

But the worst was yet to come. The rumors about the society's disloyalty to the Union had not been squelched by the earlier resolution. The abolitionists who had organized the rival missionary society continued their harsh criticism of the ACMS. In 1863, the society decided that it would put an end to these accusations once and for all. This time the society itself in session—no recess, no unofficial mass meeting—passed a stronger resolution.

> Resolved, that we unqualifiedly declare our allegiance to [the United States] government, and repudiate as false and slanderous any statements to the contrary. That we tender our sympathies to our brave and noble soldiers in the field who are defending us from the attempts of armed traitors to overthrow our government . . .

With these acts in 1861 and 1863, the American Christian Missionary Society aligned itself politically with the north. Though many church leaders in the north like Benjamin Franklin (1812-1878) had remained neutral through the war, the society had chosen sides in a political and military conflict. The man who would become the foremost church leader in the South after the Civil War, David Lipscomb (1831-1917), wrote in 1866 that the Society had committed a great wrong against the church and the cause of God. Unless there is repentance of the wrong, he asserted, "it should not receive the confidence of the Christian brotherhood."

The sectional division reflected in the missionary society gave impetus for the revival of an old journal and the creation of a new one after the war. In 1866, the *Gospel Advocate*, published in Nashville, Tennessee, and edited by Tolbert Fanning and David Lipscomb, resumed publication. The war had forced it to shut down in 1861, but Lipscomb felt it was necessary to start the *Advocate* again because there was no other paper in the movement that Southerners could read without being constantly offended by "political insinuations and slurs." Though the editors denied they intended the *Advocate* to be a sectional paper, it clearly was a southern journal—by southern leaders for southern members.

The same year the *Advocate* was reborn in Nashville, a new paper began publication in the North. A group of church and business leaders formed a publishing company to create the *Christian Standard*, a paper they believed would be more in keeping with the times. Previously, the *American Christian Review* edited by Benjamin Franklin had the most influence in the North. Unlike the leaders who formed the new company, Franklin had been neutral during the Civil War and was considered by many to be too narrow and legalistic—an "old fogy."

As was true with the *Gospel Advocate*, the sectional political feelings behind the *Christian Standard* were never part of the public explanation for starting the paper. But its sectional character was real. In 1867, David Lipscomb met Isaac Errett, the first editor of the new paper. Years later, Lipscomb reported that Errett had admitted the *Standard* was started because Franklin would not let the pro-union people publish their views on the duty of Christians to support the government in time of war.

Were We Divided by the Civil War?

The notion that anyone in America before, during, and after the Civil War could have remained unaffected by such a momentous event is remarkably naive. The war created two very different moods in the country—one in the North and one in the South—that no one could escape. Northerners had won the war. There was a general sense of victory, progress, and prosperity, mixed with a desire to punish or rehabilitate the South. Southerners had been defeated. To survive, they interpreted their defeat as discipline from God to keep them from becoming like the materialistic North and to preserve their virtues as an example of God's ideal culture.

Thus, it was not just the war but its aftermath, particularly Reconstruction in the South, that broke Christian fellowship. After the war, many churches in the prosperous northern cities became successful in society. They built large buildings with expensive stained glass. They preferred educated ministers. They could even afford expensive organs for their new buildings. Indeed, as we shall see, some opposed instrumental music in worship more for its "worldliness" than because they thought it "unscriptural." The Disciples in the North became so accepted in the culture that one of their number, James A. Garfield (1831-1881), became President of the United States.

By contrast, southern members faced starvation, disease, and economic ruin. Although some Northern church leaders made the effort to raise humanitarian support for the South, little aid actually arrived. To Southerners, it was inconceivable that their fellow Christians in the North could spend money on buildings and organs while their brothers and sisters in the South were struggling just to stay alive.

Did the Civil War divide us? It certainly did not divide us as it divided the Baptists and Methodists and Presbyterians. We did not have a central organization that represented and acted for the churches as a whole as did those bodies. We didn't have the kind of structure needed to divide that way. Nevertheless, we did have structures. We had the American Christian Missionary Society, and we had our papers. Though less formal than official assemblies and conferences, these organizations gave form to the division that had taken place in the minds and hearts of Christians in the Northern and Southern United States.

The North-South division was real and substantial. In 1906, the "official" date of the division, two-thirds of the Disciples of Christ would be in the North and two-thirds of the Churches of Christ in the South. That is too much of a coincidence for anyone to deny that the war divided us. But it was not the only matter dividing the movement. Chapter nine will discuss those other factors.

Questions for Discussion

1. Should Christians and churches become involved in the political and social issues of the day? Why or why not?

2. What do you see as the core issue for the churches of the movement regarding slavery in the period before the Civil War?

3. In what sense did the Stone-Campbell Movement avoid division during the Civil War era?

4. In what sense did the Stone-Campbell Movement divide during the Civil War era?

5. How could the division connected with the Civil War have been avoided?

6. In what ways did the Civil War era lay the foundation for other divisions that would come later?

For Further Reading

Garrett, Leroy. *The Stone-Campbell Movement*. Joplin, Missouri: College Press, 1994. See Pages 333-355.

Harrell, David Edwin, Jr. *Quest for a Christian America: The Disciples of Christ and American Society to 1866.* Nashville: Disciples of Christ Historical Society, 1966. See pages 91-138.

Maxey, Robert Tibbs. *Alexander Campbell and the Peculiar Institution*. El Paso, TX: Spanish American Evangelism, 1986.

North, James B. *Union in Truth: An Interpretive History of the Restoration Movement*. Cincinnati: Standard Publishing, 1994. See pages 227-252.

Poyner, Barry C. *Bound to Slavery: James Shannon and the Restoration Movement*. Ft. Worth: Star Bible Publications, 1999.

CHAPTER 9

Issues and Editors

Isaac Errett

How does one unite movements that have no organization beyond the congregations? That was the question in 1832 when the Stone and Campbell Movements came together. The answer then was two-fold: congregation by congregation through the work of traveling preachers and through the influence of religious papers. How does a congregational movement divide? Moses Lard and others believed the Disciples could not divide because they didn't have the denominational structure to formalize a division. As we saw in the last chapter, the Missionary Society somewhat fulfilled this role as churches supported or opposed it. But fundamentally we divided as we united, congregation by congregation, through the influence of religious editors and powerful preachers.

What issues divided us? Again, slavery, the Civil War, and Reconstruction were among the causes of division. The war and its consequences shaped the discussion of the religious issues in the division—the Missionary Society and instrumental music—as well as the approaches to biblical interpretation that stood behind those religious issues.

Opposition to the Missionary Society

When the American Christian Missionary Society formed in Cincinnati in 1849, it encountered little opposition from preachers

Tolbert Fanning

and editors in the church. Two of those who were later most vehement in their opposition—Tolbert Fanning and Benjamin Franklin—had even once served as officers of the Society.

Fanning was the first to break with the Society. When he began the *Gospel Advocate* in 1855, one purpose of the journal was to give the "Society issue" a thorough discussion. By 1857, Fanning was convinced that the Society was not authorized by Scripture. Yet he refused at this point to break fellowship with those who supported the Society. He even addressed the Society's annual meeting in 1859 rejoicing that the movement was still united. It was only after the Society's pro-Union resolutions in 1861 and 1863 that Fanning began to make the Society a matter of fellowship.

The same pattern holds with Benjamin Franklin, who edited the popular religious paper the *American Christian Review* published in Cincinnati, the headquarters of the Society. Franklin served as a secretary for the Society for thirteen years, but in 1866 turned completely against it. Although from the North, he also was scandalized by the Society's abandonment of neutrality and pacifism during the war.

The arguments against the Society were generally consistent among those who opposed it. It had become involved in sectional politics. It was an inefficient way to do mission work. It dictated to the churches. The most telling argument was the silence of the Bible on church organization beyond the local congregation. Those who supported the Society took that silence as permission. Those who opposed it believed silence prohibited the formation of a missionary society.

A compromise plan for cooperation among congregations for missions, the Louisville plan, was proposed in 1868, but failed after a few years. Eventually most preachers and papers in the North, including the influential *Christian Standard*, supported the Missionary Society and other organizations for benevolent and missions work. Those in the South generally opposed any organization beyond the local congregation.

Instrumental Music in Worship

Discussion of the propriety of using instrumental music in worship was not unique to us. Zwingli and Calvin had opposed the practice during the Reformation. In America, Congregational churches did not use instruments in worship until after the Revolutionary War. The issue did not appear in the early history of our movement, perhaps because few frontier churches could afford instruments. The first recorded instance of an instrument used in worship among the Stone-Campbell churches was in Midway, Kentucky, in 1859. The minister, L.L. Pinkerton (1812-1875), brought in a melodeon to help singing that was so bad it "scared even the rats from worship."

Only after the Civil War did many churches bring in instruments. Those who did argued that they were aids to singing and appealed to a new generation of worshippers. Opposition to instruments came primarily, but not exclusively, from the South. Part of that opposition was social and economic: how could northern churches waste money on organs while their southern brothers and sisters starved? Others argued that the use of instruments put too much emphasis on the beauty of the music to the neglect of glorifying God. Their use did not promote spiritual worship.

As with the Missionary Society, the primary objection to instrumental music in worship came from the silence of Scripture. Since the New Testament mentioned singing but not instruments in worship, instruments were prohibited. On the other hand, those who supported their use argued that silence permitted instruments as an aid to singing just as silence permitted song books, song leaders, and church buildings as aids to worship. Interestingly, some applied the argument from silence differently to the issues. Thus, prominent leaders such as J.W. McGarvey (1829-1911) and Moses Lard supported the Missionary Society, but opposed instruments in worship.

Why was the instrumental music issue so divisive? Perhaps because it was so visible. One could worship for years with a congregation and not know which members disagreed with your position on Missionary Societies and other issues. One could see immediately on entering a church building whether or not that congregation used instrumental music.

Although many leaders tried for a while to avoid making the instrument a matter of fellowship, it soon became one. After all, what could those conscientiously opposed to instruments do when one was introduced into their congregation? It seemed to most that they had no choice but to form a separate church.

Steps Toward Division

There were other divisive issues discussed during this time such as who should be allowed to partake of communion and the role of ministers. In spite of the disagreement on these and on instrumental music and the Missionary Society, there was still something of an uneasy unity through the 1870s. By the 1880s, however, some were calling for recognition of a division they claimed had already occurred.

Chief among those was Daniel Sommer (1850-1940), who had followed Benjamin Franklin as editor of the *American Christian Review*. Sommer saw the changes among the churches during the previous thirty years as examples of apostasy. He made a distinction between "the Church of Christ" and the "so-called Christian Church." In 1889, an elder at Sand Creek, Illinois, read Sommer's "An Address and Declaration" (apparently a play on Thomas Campbell's *Declaration and Address*), outlining his plan to save the movement from "innovations and corruptions." If leaders and churches would not give up practices such as instrumental music, support of the Society, located preachers, and others, then Sommer said "we cannot and will not regard them as brethren."

Most leaders in both the North and the South were not as quick as Sommer to proclaim a division. Eventually, though, they had to admit it. For many years, David Lipscomb was extremely reluctant to acknowledge the division. By 1904, however, he was compiling a list of faithful churches and preachers, another way that a congregational movement identifies a split. In 1907, when asked by the Director of the Bureau of the Census if he should list

David Lipscomb

Churches of Christ separately from Disciples of Christ, Lipscomb painfully agreed that they were now two distinct bodies.

Unity or Division?

Certainly the story of this and subsequent divisions is one of the most embarrassing parts of our heritage. How could a group that began as a unity movement later fracture and splinter? How could significant differences between the Stone and Campbell groups be overcome for the sake of unity in 1832, while seemingly less important issues divide us by 1906?

At least part of the answer to those questions lies in attitude. Certainly, particular doctrines must be maintained to be faithful to God. The New Testament is greatly concerned with doctrinal purity. But the doctrines at the heart of the gospel always center on Christ. The issues that usually divide us do not. How can that be? Because we make those issues more important and divisive than they should be.

Even in the decades following the Civil War some refused to split with their brothers and sisters over the issues and the ill feelings caused by the war. One such man was T.B. Larimore (1843-1929). Born in poverty in east Tennessee, Larimore was baptized in Kentucky in 1864 and later attended Franklin College near Nashville, studying under Tolbert Fanning. Larimore spent the rest of his life as an educator and traveling evangelist, operating Mars Hill Academy near Florence, Alabama from 1871 to 1887.

Thus, Larimore was a loyal son of the South, influenced by some of the strongest opponents of the Missionary Society and instrumental music in worship. He personally never supported either practice. However, he refused to declare himself publicly on these issues because he believed the body of Christ should not divide over such matters. He saw his duty as a Christian evangelist to proclaim the good news of the New Testament. He had nothing to do with those questions over which "the wisest and best of men disagreed."

He certainly was successful in his evangelistic work, baptizing over 10,000 people in his lifetime. But he was under intense pressure to take sides in the division. It exasperated many that he

T.B. Larimore

would not line up with either side. Partisans on both sides criticized him harshly, but he consistently refused to defend himself. The only way to avoid division, he thought, was to allow freedom in matters of opinion.

In this regard, Larimore reflected the heritage of Thomas Campbell and the *Declaration and Address*. When Campbell spoke of "being silent where the Bible is silent," he allowed for strong opinions on what that silence meant. Some might think silence permits; others might be sure it forbids. The "silence" Campbell called for was the refusal to make those opinions divisive matters of faith.

Many in Churches of Christ turned Campbell's teaching upside down, insisting that "being silent" meant prohibiting any practice not mentioned in the New Testament. They even went farther and refused fellowship to those who approved of those practices. This is what Larimore would not do. He would not break relations with those who were (in his opinion) wrong on the issues.

Larimore's fellowship with Disciples of Christ and Churches of Christ was in deed, not just in word. He continued to preach wherever he was invited, and was on the List of Preachers in the Disciples Yearbook until 1925. He wrote for religious papers in both groups. He spoke well of all. In his words:

> I never call Christians or others "anti's," "digressives," "mossbacks," "tackies," or "trash." I concede to all, and accord to all, the same sincerity and courtesy I claim for myself, as the Golden Rule demands….

Some in his day and in ours would say that such an attitude would lead the church into wholesale false teaching. Instead, if everyone in his day had imitated his attitude, the "issues" would never have divided us. In any age, it seems like a good idea to follow the Golden Rule, to think the best of fellow Christians, to pray more and dispute less. That is the legacy of Larimore.

Questions for Discussion

1. How did post-Civil War conditions affect the discussion over the Missionary Society and instrumental music? Are there ever any "pure" discussions of doctrinal issues or do circumstances always color our thinking?

2. Would supporting a missionary society be an issue in your congregation today? Why or why not?

3. What are some good arguments for acappella music in worship? What are some bad arguments for it?

4. Can we fellowship others who disagree with us on these issues? On other issues? What would that fellowship look like?

5. Would following the Golden Rule eliminate our doctrinal differences with other Christians? Would it help our relations with them?

For Further Reading

Foster, Douglas A. *Will the Cycle Be Unbroken? Churches of Christ Face the 21st Century* (Abilene: ACU Press, 1994). See Pages 147-159.

Garrett, Leroy. *The Stone-Campbell Movement*. Joplin, Missouri: College Press, 1994. See Pages 381-405.

McAllister, Lester G. and Tucker, William E. *Journey in Faith*. Saint Louis, Chalice Press, 1975. See Pages 233-254.

Webb, Henry E. *In Search of Christian Unity: A History of the Restoration Movement*, revised edition. Abilene, TX: ACU Press, 2003. See Pages 193-218.

West, Earl Irvin. *The Search for the Ancient Order*, Vol. 1. Nashville: Gospel Advocate, 1986. See pages 306-317.

1907-1949: Growth and Yet Further Division

Some of the spirit of T.B. Larimore lived on as folk from Christian Churches and Churches of Christ met in a "Centennial Convention" in Pittsburgh in 1909 to celebrate Thomas Campbell's 1809 *Declaration and Address*. Disciples of Christ, as the people of these churches were still known in the early 1900s, were an optimistic lot; their numbers had grown five-fold between 1860 and 1900 to about a million people in the United States. A great gathering of an estimated 20,000 at Forbes Field celebrated Communion together, and the steamship Oregon, a gift of the Oregon churches, was launched during the convention to be used in missionary work along the Congo river. Some of those who attended were from the Churches of Christ, despite their new separate listing in the Census of 1906; for example, the great teacher J. W. McGarvey of Lexington's College of the Bible was among the attendees.

But this celebratory and optimistic gathering took place just as new issues and events would usher in new difficulties for the people of the Stone-Campbell movement. The movement's congregations would continue to grow, to nearly two million members by the mid-twentieth-century, and new educational and other ministries would blossom, but all of this was accompanied by divisive and disheartening developments. Parts of this story are not easy to write or, for that matter, to read about. Other parts of this narrative tell us about things from which we still benefit.

Steamship *Oregon*

New Issues and Developments

Christian Churches/Churches of Christ/Disciples of Christ had entered fervently into cross-cultural missions in the late 1800s. The American Christian Missionary Society (1849) was joined by the Christian Women's Board of Missions in 1874, led by Caroline Neville Pearre; the *Christian Standard's* Isaac Errett urged the churches to "Help Those Women." The men joined the effort in 1875 with the Foreign Christian Missionary Society. In 1919 the ACMS, the CWBM, and the FCMS merged to create the United Christian Missionary Society (UCMS). Missionaries were active in Jamaica, China, the Philippines and the Belgian Congo, among other places. Others, like W. D. Cunningham in Japan in the early 1900s, were "direct support" missionaries, working outside the organized societies.

As a venue for reporting on these and other evangelistic and social agencies, the annual gathering of Disciples became, in 1917, the International Convention of the Disciples of Christ. A small representative body, the Committee on Recommendations, would prepare an agenda for the mass convention. Then, in the larger sessions, all attendees could participate and vote on the committee's recommendations.

But Christian Churches were a part of the larger American church scene. New issues were spurring debate among Christians of all denominations. The impact of a movement for more "scientific" or "higher" forms of biblical criticism gave birth to an ideology commonly called modernism or liberalism. Against this theological ideology rose fundamentalism, which in its more extreme forms argued for reading the Bible literally and affirming that the scriptures were "inerrant" (though there was no absolute agreement about what this actually meant).

The great majority of people in the pews of Christian Churches and Churches of Christ probably did not fit comfortably into either of these camps, particularly into the more extreme parts of these movements. They sought to be faithful to scripture. They would have appreciated Alexander Campbell's rules for scripture interpretation, written in the 1830s, which called for a thoughtful and intelligent handling of the authoritative apostolic teachings of the New Testament.

But it was perhaps inevitable that we could not remain untouched by these issues. We were not an isolationist movement. Future teachers in our colleges took degrees from places favorable to modernism, like the University of Chicago or Yale University. Some enthusiastically carried this modernist teaching onto the faculties of our schools (in Kentucky, the College of the Bible's trustees held hearings about the faculty's theology); others rejected these higher criticisms and found venues for teaching a more conservative approach to scripture (Cincinnati Bible Seminary, seeing modernism as a destructive influence on the churches, began its work in 1924).

Another issue rising in the early part of the 1900s was the Federated Church movement (more commonly known now as the Ecumenical Movement). With a desire for Christian unity, the Federal Council of Churches (later the National Council of Churches) came into being in the first decade of the 1900s.

From the time of Barton Stone and the *Last Will and Testament* and Thomas Campbell's *Declaration and Address*, we were a people historically dedicated to Christian unity. But what exactly does this mean? Dialogue? Comity agreements (where denominations negotiate about where they may and may not establish work)? Merger of denominations? Or…? Some Disciples entered into this movement whole-heartedly; others saw potential in its intent, but were nervous about the way it would work. Others totally rejected any involvement with ecumenism.

For some Disciples—a minority through the first half of the 1900s—one way to manifest unity with other professing Christians outside our movement was to practice "open membership." While there was agreement that all Christians are "members of the Body" of Christ, the advocates of open membership extended their thinking to include the American cultural practice of local church "membership": all Christians, they said, including the "pious unimmersed" (recipients of infant baptism) should be accepted as members of Christian Churches. That would allow their participation in congregational decision-making, voting, holding office, teaching, etc., though not baptized in a manner consistent with the congregation's historic teaching and practice.

While only a small number of congregations adopted this practice before World War II, tensions arose regarding the practice of open membership by UCMS missionaries on the foreign field, specifically in China and the Philippines. The International Convention passed resolutions in 1920, 1922, and 1925 that took a stand against this practice by the Society, and these resolutions reflected the overwhelming majority of our churches at that time. But when the Convention at Memphis in 1926, a very controversial convention, at best, accepted a special report from a committee of the UCMS saying that the Society had taken care of matters on the field, a division among the Disciples that was already bubbling under the surface began to come out into the open. Many conservative Disciples had for some time been losing confidence in the UCMS, and in the ability of the International Convention to be an effective forum for their concerns. The Memphis convention was one of several watershed events that served as a harbinger of a second division in the history of the movement.

Those who continued to cooperate with the UCMS (and the convention as the venue for its reports) were dubbed "Cooperatives." Congregations and individuals who now chose to work independently of the society and the convention were nicknamed "Independents."

"Independents" for the most part were not opposed to working cooperatively. They would join with other congregations to support evangelistic agencies, church camps, homes for children and the aged, and even foreign missions (like the later Christian Missionary Fellowship). But, rightly or wrongly, they had lost faith in the UCMS and the International Convention, and began to move toward a separate identity from the "Cooperative Disciples." As the twentieth century went on, the name "Disciples" would come to be associated with the Cooperatives, and some Independents intentionally disassociated Christian Churches and Churches of Christ from the historic "Disciples" term for the people of the movement.

Edwin Errett

This emerging group separate from Cooperative Disciples established a new venue for preaching and fellowship: the North American Christian Convention had its first meeting in 1927. Originally it was intended to be a meeting place for people across the movement. The preaching and fellowship did not include society business meetings or any passing of resolutions. But as time went on, the North American convention came to be identified almost exclusively with the "Independents." Independent Disciples were on the way to becoming an identifiable fellowship of Christian Churches and Churches of Christ.

These congregations independent of the UCMS and the Disciples of Christ were the theologically more "conservative" part of the movement, while the Cooperatives were relatively more open to "liberal" or "modernist" theology (the words "liberal" and "conservative" are, of course, problematic in some ways, and at times neither helpful or even very accurate; they are offered here as simple generalizations). And from congregation to congregation there was, of course, variety within both the "Cooperatives" and the "Independents."

Efforts to Preserve Unity

More than one historian in our movement has made the observation that divisions among us are not a one-time event but a drawn-out process. Despite the issues of modernism, open membership, and ecumenical relationships, efforts were made to preserve the movement's unity.

Indeed, many congregations and individuals were not exclusively Cooperative or Independent. Edwin Errett, editor (1929-44) of the *Christian Standard*, favored agencies like the National Benevolent Association (homes for the aged and children) and the Pension Fund, related to the Cooperatives. But at the same time he chose not to support open membership and the UCMS. He represented the movement at ecumenical gatherings, as in Edinburgh, Scotland, in 1937.

Errett participated in a *Commission on Restudy* of the Disciples alongside a wide variety of the movement's leaders from 1934-49. The commission attempted to discover where common ground or

Frederick Doyle Kershner

differences existed among Christian Churches on a variety of important issues: unity and restoration; denomination or movement; the role of conventions; local church autonomy; the New Testament church. In its meetings there was a sense of respect and fellowship across the lines of the issues. But sadly, the forces of division were too strong and the commission's efforts came to an inconclusive end in 1949.

Other people also worked to keep the lines of communication open within the movement. The Butler University School of Religion, led by Dean Frederick Doyle Kershner from 1924-44, drew students from a wide variety within the movement. The seminary's graduates contributed to both Cooperative and Independent endeavors.

The churches in Oregon are another example. For many decades since the troubles of the 1920s the Oregon Christian Convention has been a place for fellowship across the movement's separations.

There were other heartening developments as well. The World Convention of the Churches of Christ, embracing all parts of our movement in the USA and around the world, first met in 1930 at

Jesse Bader

James Murch

the National City Christian Church in Washington, D.C. Jesse M. Bader was the driving force behind the WCCC, a gathering that continues to bring fellowship among Stone-Campbell churches right to the present. The Pension Fund began in the Thirties as well, and is still serving church workers across the lines of division within the movement. In that same decade Claude E. Witty of Detroit, a minister among the Churches of Christ, and James DeForest Murch from the Christian Churches, initiated rallies for fellowship at a time when such meetings were not in vogue.

And all the while, there were ministers and educators who continued to attend and enjoy fellowship with both the International Convention and the North American Christian Convention. Through the 1940s there were congregations whose outreach giving mirrored Edwin Errett's convictions and his irenic spirit.

Choosing Paths Of Separation

Despite the efforts of some to bridge the differences among Disciples, the momentum toward separation gained the upper hand among both Cooperatives and Independents in the decade of the Forties. The lines were hardening and the distinctions were becoming, for many congregations, matters of identification with one group or the other. Many of us willed the division in the movement, preferring separation from other sub-groups of the movement. Others of us accepted it, unhappy about it but with a sense of resignation. Still others of us endeavored to keep the lines of communication open.

Congregations, as they determined to whom their financial outreach giving would go, moved toward a separation. As they chose the missionaries, colleges or seminaries, church camps, retirement homes, conventions, and other ministries to support, congregations were increasingly identified with the "Cooperative" or "Independent" labels. The choice of journals and educational materials was likewise a clue to group relationship: Independents chose the Standard Publishing Company's materials, while Cooperatives chose the Christian Board of Publication. Cooperatives sent their missions money to the UCMS, while Independents supported missionaries with "direct support" funds rather than through a missionary society.

Independent Disciples had founded, by 1949, more than thirty Bible Colleges to train preachers, shunning the older Disciple colleges and seminaries that were increasingly seen as too "liberal." The new Bible colleges alongside Cincinnati Bible Seminary included, among others, Atlanta Christian College, Lincoln Bible Institute, Ozark Bible College, Great Lakes Bible College, Manhattan Bible College, Boise Bible College, and Nebraska Christian College. They joined older institutions for training preachers like Johnson Bible College (1893), Northwest Christian College (1895), Minnesota Bible College (1913) and Kentucky Christian College (1919). These institutions, albeit with some name changes, are still serving the movement. One historic liberal arts institution, Milligan College (1880), also identified primarily with the independent churches.

AN EMERGING IDENTITY: *CHRISTIAN CHURCHES AND CHURCHES OF CHRIST*

The first half of the twentieth century, then, opened with enthusiastic promise and yet with troublesome new issues. We can celebrate continued growth of numbers and churches, the establishment of colleges and other institutions that still serve the movement, and the persistence of those whose irenic spirits wanted to maintain a broad fellowship.

But by the middle of the century, two groups of Christian Churches were being identified as separate fellowships. The "Cooperatives" and the International Convention of the Disciples of Christ would, in the next two decades, evolve their distinctive structures and identity. A Commission on Restructure resulted in the formal adoption in 1968 of a provisional design for a denomination to be known as the "Christian Church (Disciples of Christ)." The term Cooperatives soon faded away, replaced by the term "Disciples of Christ" for this part of the Stone-Campbell heritage.

Those choosing to work independently were assuming a distinctive identity as well. Served by the North American Christian Convention and an array of new colleges and social service agencies, "Christian Churches and Churches of Christ" were increasingly identified as one of the three major subsets of the Stone-Campbell Movement, along with the Churches of Christ and the Disciples of Christ.

Division is never a pleasant memory, and it is a further embarrassment for a movement dedicated to Christian unity. There was a tendency on both sides to assign the blame for which group had broken away from the other. At the same time, of course, there had been growth and many good developments in the first half of the century as well and we can be justifiably proud of them. The reality was, however, that by 1949 Christian Churches and Churches of Christ were poised for a new half-century of growth and development as a distinctive entity in both the movement and in the wider church.

Questions for Discussion:

I. Is "cooperation" among the congregations of our movement a good thing? If so, what are its advantages? Its limitations? In what ways does my own local church cooperate with other congregations of the Stone-Campbell movement?

2. What convictions are worth a congregation's taking a stand? On scripture? On the ordinances (baptism and the Lord's Supper)? On...? Can our congregation have fellowship with another Christian Church or Church of Christ with whom it disagrees?

3. In light of the movement's second division in the twentieth century, is "division" always bad? Is it bad, but necessary? Is it sometimes good? How do these questions relate to the answers we give for question #2?

4. Does a congregation have to practice "open membership" in order to affirm that there are Christians outside the Stone/Campbell movement? What other creative and intentional ways are there to make such an affirmation without weakening our understandings and practices regarding Christian baptism?

5. Is it surprising that this second division (among Christian Churches) took place? Or should it be seen as predictable in light of wider developments in the Church?

For Further Reading:

Garrett, Leroy. *The Stone-Campbell Movemen*t. Joplin, MO: College Press, 1994.See pages 407-32.

McAllister, Lester G., and Tucker, William E. *Journey in Faith: A History of the Christian Church (Disciples of Christ)*. St. Louis: Chalice Press, 1975. See pages 360-386.

North, James. *Union in Truth: An Interpretive History of the Restoration Movement*. Cincinnati: Standard Publishing Company, 1994. See pages 255-352.

Webb, Henry. *In Search of Christian Unity: A History of the Restoration Movement*. Abilene: Abilene Christian University Press, 2003. See pages 239-354.

CHAPTER 11

1950-1990: Christian Churches and Churches of Christ—Identity and Activity

We have noted that it is difficult to fix a date for the emergence of Christian Churches and Churches of Christ (CC/CC) as a distinctive segment of the historic Stone-Campbell Movement, alongside the Churches of Christ and the Christian Church (Disciples of Christ). Some cite the Memphis convention of 1926; some would point to the growing estrangement of Independents and Cooperatives during the 1940s as the time when these two groups began to emerge with separate identities.

The Stone-Campbell Movement, despite its history of a desire for Christian unity, had experienced, sad to say, yet a second parting of the ways. However we might interpret the developments that led to the distinctive identity of Christian Churches and Churches of Christ, the fact is that the decades from 1950-1990 would see an outpouring of energy and growth in this identifiable segment of the movement.

Growth and Institutional Development

One sign that Christian Churches and Churches of Christ had emerged with a distinctive identity came in 1955: a new *Directory of the Ministry* listed congregations and church workers who were no longer identified with the *Yearbook* of the Cooperative Disciples. By the mid-Fifties the Disciples initiated activities that would, in 1968, "restructure" the voluntary cooperation of those congregations into a denomination known as the Christian Church (Disciples of Christ).

The "Independents," as some continue to call Christian Churches and Churches of Christ, were busy establishing and growing new cooperative (small "c") ventures of their own. Among those ventures was an unofficial, but important, venue for gathering.

The North American Christian Convention, born in 1927 and meeting annually since 1950, experienced a tremendous growth in these decades. From 1,735 registrations in 1950 and 4,480 in 1960, those registering for the convention rose to 42,195 in 1970 and by 1979 to 57, 330. Coordinating the details of these increasingly large gatherings was the Director of the North American Christian Convention, Leonard Wymore, who held this post from 1963 to 1986. The 1986 convention in Indianapolis celebrated the Lord's Supper in the Hoosier Dome with 40,000 in attendance (a conservative estimate—-the more generous was 50,000).

This growth was further encouraged by the development of the "Bible Bowl" competition at the convention. Beginning in 1965, congregational teams of youth from around the country brought their enthusiastic presence to the NACC.

The NACC had become, in these years, a venue of great importance for Christian Churches and Churches of Christ. Although doing no official business for the movement (only a short session to elect the convention's "Continuation Committee"), the convention was a gathering for fellowship, preaching, workshops, and mutual encouragement. Colleges, missionary groups, and social agencies were given opportunities for promoting their work in an exhibit area. Thousands went home refreshed and with new incentive for the work of their own congregations. The NACC was both a reflection of, and an encourager of, significant growth and vitality in the movement's churches during these decades.

Leonard Wymore

Other conventions complemented the work of the NACC. Some were state conventions, as in Wisconsin, or conventions for teens, as in Tennessee. "Annual Meetings" of churches in a given area still provide fellowship for the churches as well, the oldest being the East Tennessee/Western North Carolina annual meeting that dates back to 1829. For a people without official ecclesiastical structures beyond the local congregation, many such gatherings were ad hoc in nature, and this was reflected also in a series of "Open Forums" held in the late 1980s for the purpose of examining the ideas of the movement.

Meeting jointly with the NACC in 1986 was another gathering of Christians focused specifically on missions. The National Missionary Convention met first in 1948, and annually after 1950. The increasing significance of the NMC from the Fifties to the present reflects the growth of foreign and domestic missions supported by Christian Churches and Churches of Christ.

To illustrate this growth it is interesting to compare the listing of foreign missions and missionaries in the *Directory of the Ministry* for 1955 (its first year) with the 1992 issue. From a total of about 250 missionaries (counting both spouses of married couples in the total) in just over twenty countries, Christian Churches and Churches of Christ were supporting over a thousand foreign missionaries in about 64 countries in 1992. Whether through mission agencies like the Christian Missionary Fellowship (1949), Pioneer Bible Translators (1976), or through services for other missionary groups and direct-support missionaries by the Mission Services Association (1946), the work of cross-cultural evangelism grew significantly during this era.

It is difficult, in a concise history, to do justice to the great growth of domestic work among Christian Churches and Churches of Christ in these decades. Evangelism and new church planting organizations, like the Chicago District Evangelizing Association, among many others, came into being around the country. These efforts employed the "church growth" strategies of researchers like Donald McGavran. Some of the Bible colleges worked closely with these church planting efforts. Accompanying these efforts was the popularity of new worship

Dean Walker

Doug Dickey

styles that were seen to appeal to many Americans, and a willingness to use progressive and pragmatic tools for growth. Congregational staffs began to include Youth and Children's ministers as a way of building for the future.

One of the significant developments of these decades was the establishment of campus ministries at public universities. Doug Dickey not only built a sizeable and vibrant work at Purdue University, but he and his students gave encouragement to new ministries on other campuses as well. Regional retreats bringing together students from across the Midwest offered teaching and fellowship for these programs.

At the same time, Christian Churches and Churches of Christ were financially supporting the relatively new development of Bible colleges (see Chapter 10), and looked to these institutions for a new generation of preachers and other church workers. In addition, a liberal arts institution, Milligan College (from 1880), also served the movement, and experienced significant growth under its President, Dean Everest Walker (1950-67) and his successors. Graduate seminaries also developed in the Fifties and Sixties to serve the churches: Cincinnati Bible Seminary, Emmanuel School of Religion, and Lincoln Christian Seminary.

During this era the cooperative efforts of congregations and individuals led to church-supported homes for the aged, children's homes, and other social ministries. Older church camps and conference centers were improved, and new ones were opened. It is probably fair to say that for Christian Churches and Churches of Christ, in this era, being "independent" could also include a commitment to a lot of voluntary cooperation.

The Restoration Agenda

The history of the Stone-Campbell Movement has always focused primarily on the nature of the Lord's Church. This focus called for the *unity* of Christ's body. It called for the *restoration* of New Testament Christianity. Both of these were seen as means to the end that the world might believe, as means toward the *mission* of the church (evangelism).

In retrospect, Christian Churches and Churches of Christ, in the era under consideration in this chapter, appeared to stress most heavily the restoration part of the movement's agenda. While evangelism was certainly our ultimate goal, the emphasis on the restoration motif is seen first and foremost in the nomenclature we used for ourselves: "The Restoration Movement."

This emphasis on restoration manifested itself in a strong stand regarding weekly communion, the practice of believers' immersion, and the local governance of elders and deacons in a free congregation.

But what did we mean by "restoration"? For some, it meant that the first-century churches provided a blueprint to be reproduced. It was as if the New Testament era was a golden age to be replicated, a pattern for our own age. Any intervening church history since that time had no normative authority for us, and some appeared to believe that the church ceased to exist, early in the second century, until the restoration took place in the early nineteenth century. As a golden age and pattern, the absence of missionary societies in the first century meant we need not, indeed should not, have them now.

To the degree that this view of restoration prevailed among us, Christian Churches and Churches of Christ were tempted toward what some came to describe as "patternism." Restoring the New Testament pattern could take on the appearance of legalism, using the New Testament scriptures like the Boy Scout Handbook (which tells us how to tie all of the various knots). As time passed, this view of restoration has become uncomfortable for some.

Others among us, also concerned for restoration, took the point of view that what we seek is a restoration of the church that was in the mind of Christ and which is reflected in the apostolic writings. This mind is found in scripture, not as a legalistic pattern but as a call to building up the body of Christ in unity, knowledge, and maturity. Just as the churches in the New Testament were called on to reform (the church in Corinth, for example, in I Corinthians 1), so should all churches, in our age as well, seek to be continually reforming. The attitude of always reforming (*semper reformanda*) means that restoration is never, on this earth, fully achieved.

Whatever the definition of restoration, the emphasis on that motif often meant only a scant attention to the goal of unity. Some of us saw unity simply as the product of agreeing on the agenda of restoration. Once we were all in the properly restored pattern, then there would be unity.

But again, what was the definition of "unity?" Would it exist only when all Christians agreed on all matters of doctrine, a confessional conformity, so to speak? Or would it be an institutional cohesion within a structural arrangement, a form of conformity-in-a-corporation? Thomas Campbell's *Declaration and Address* in 1809, written to address the need for unity in the church of Christ, does not appear to have been comfortable with these institutional or doctrinal definitions.

Christian Churches and Churches of Christ, given our congregational nature, have had to be creative and intentional about pursuing the unity motif of our movement. And it was Campbell's alternative that was invoked in at least one major instance during this era. In 1988, at a meeting of an "Open Forum" in Indianapolis, a Disciples of Christ speaker, Michael Kinnamon, challenged the participants to find a visible expression of their desire for unity within Christ's church. The result was a series of discussions held over the next few years by concerned persons from Christian Churches and Churches of Christ with representatives from the Commission on Christian Unity of the Church of God (Anderson, Indiana). Papers by Henry Webb (Milligan College), James North (Cincinnati Christian Seminary), and others were read and discussed alongside similar offerings from the Church of God. In some localities this produced intentional opportunities for cooperative worship and work between congregations of the two groups.

Henery Webb

The unity motif can find expression in any congregation's locality, of course, and it has depended on a local commitment for its implementation. For Christian Churches and Churches of Christ in this era (1950-1990), there was a wide variety of activity (or, in truth, inactivity) in pursuit of unity with Christians outside of our movement.

A Cultural Movement?

The Lord's church always lives within a cultural context, as do the movements that serve the church. Christian Churches and Churches of Christ are no exception. We were historically a movement of plain, simple, and rational lower-middle to middle-class folk. The Post-WWII decades, with the GI Bill and the economic prosperity of these years, strengthened the country's middle class. And this was reflected in our movement. We were becoming more solidly middle-to-upper-middle class, particularly as we assertively planted churches in the prosperous suburbs of the expanding cities.

As the social, political, and economic climate of the country in general became more conservative in the late Seventies,

Eighties, and Nineties, our churches were, on the whole, at home with the larger culture. On the theological continuum of American Christianity, we were already a relatively conservative group. That theological conservatism had variety, to be sure. Some of us reflected more resolutely the patternism mentioned earlier, while others were somewhat more moderate. This in turn affected our willingness to participate in activities with Christians outside our movement, as noted earlier in this chapter.

While willing, then, to be very progressive in methodologies of church growth, worship, and programming, we reflected at the same time the developing conservative mood of the United States, and were reasonably comfortable in this culture.

In some respects our comfort with American culture was not so commendable. We were not among the leaders in responding to the Civil Right Movement. This uneven response was illustrated in 1968 when the Board of First Christian Church of Nashville, Tennessee, passed a resolution "...to refuse admittance of Negroes to church worship." At the same time, African American preachers like Bill Ellis were invited to address the NACC, and his daughter was among the first to finally integrate Milligan College in the late Sixties.

The decades of the Fifties to the early Nineties were years when Christian Churches and Churches of Christ emerged with a clearer identity among Christian movements in the United States and within the Stone/Campbell heritage. Thoughtful observers may give mixed reviews to us in this era, but it was certainly not a boring or inconsequential time period.

Questions for Discussion:

1. "Christian Churches and Churches of Christ." "Christian Church (Disciples of Christ)." "Churches of Christ." Do you have difficulty explaining this set of terminology to your friends? Is this a price we pay for emerging with a distinctive identity?

2. What might be the significance of using a title in the singular for Christian Churches and Churches of Christ (our branch of the movement, as in "The Christian Church?" or "The Churches of Christ?")? Or should the singular be reserved for use as a reference to the church universal?

3. What contributions to the emerging identity of Christian Churches and Churches of Christ (as a distinct segment of the Stone-Campbell movement) come to us from the service and ministry tools among us? (the North American Christian Convention, the National Missionary Convention, missions agencies, Bible and Liberal Arts colleges, seminaries, publishers, etc.)

4. How has "restoration and unity unto mission" been taught in our congregations? Have we done a good job of teaching these parts of our movement's agenda? Are we doing a good job of teaching them to the younger generations in our churches?

5. How is our movement reflective of the cultural context in which it lives? On the other hand, how are we counter-cultural?

For Further Reading:

Dickey, Douglas A. *Campus Ministry*. Joplin, MO: College Press, 1994.

Garrett, Leroy. *The Stone-Campbell Movement*. Joplin, MO: College Press, 1994. See pages 469-487.

Hayden, Edwin V. *North American Gold: The Story of Fifty North American* Conventions. Joplin, MO: College Press, 1989.

Webb, Henry E. *In Search of Christian Unity: A History of the Restoration Movement.* 2nd Edition. Abilene, TX: ACU Press, 2003. See pages 355-387, 421-435.

CHAPTER 12

1990-Present: Growth and Identity Crisis

By the early Nineties, Christian Churches and Churches of Christ were an identifiable and growing fellowship of congregations on the North American church scene, both within the Stone-Campbell Movement and within the wider church. New congregations were being planted, especially in the suburbs of our large cities, and the techniques of the church growth movement were being successfully employed. The colleges and seminaries were growing as well, and most of them were moving toward regional and national accreditation standards. Missions programs, domestic and cross-cultural, were continuing to flourish.

And the growth had not yet reached its peak. But at the same time, our congregations were experiencing a time of re-assessment about our identity and our place in the wider church. Recent decades have not been exactly dull.

Numerical And Congregational Growth

A report released in 2002 by the Glenmary Research Center, a Roman Catholic study group (cited in the *Christian Standard*, Nov. 3, 2002, p. 899) reported that the two fastest growing church groups (percentage-wise) in the decade from 1990 to 2000 were the Latter Day Saints (Mormons) and Christian Churches and Churches of Christ. The latter, the study reported, had grown by 18.6% during the Nineties to a membership conservatively estimated at 1.2 million.

Lynn Gardner, in a *Christian Standard* article early in 2008, acknowledged this research and raised the question of why our movement of churches had been so blessed of God with such growth. It's a fair-enough question.

Perhaps, in an age that is often called "post-denominational," our plea seems to match this prevailing church culture. We use a generic nomenclature: Christian; church of Christ. Our congregations do not insist on required denominational loyalties to an institutional headquarters. Thus, as mobile Americans move freely about the country and are not necessarily wedded to past denominational ties, they find our nomenclature and church polity appealing. They are, perhaps, looking instead for a sense of community, for a congregation with a vital ministry of teaching and social activity for their children, or a style of worship that is different from the churches from which they come.

We debate about these things among ourselves, of course. Are we choosing music or programming that is attractive to newcomers? Is it that we have, perhaps more successfully than other Christian groups, learned how to "market" the church by the way we do things? Marketing is, after all, a feature of life in almost every phase of the American consumer culture. And if we have employed such strategies, is this bad, especially if it reaches people for Christ? It is certainly fair to say that all of us want the Lord's church to grow, and the strategies used are a great topic of discussion.

Perhaps one reason we have grown is our tradition of seeking "catholicity." The word "catholic" (with a lower case "c") means universal, and we have sought to be just that, not seeking to be unique or different. Vincent of Lerins, in the fifth century, defined catholic as that which is believed in all times and all places by all people. We use universal names like Christian; we use the twenty-seven books of the New Testament recognized universally, as canonical, by all Christians; we practice ordinances that are universally observed by all Christians—baptism and the Lord's Supper. Denominations are often known by their unique names (after a person, a polity, or a doctrine), by their distinctive theologies, or by beliefs and practices that are uniquely associated with that particular group. For Christian Churches and Churches of Christ, however, it may be that the growth discovered in the 2002 study has been encouraged to the extent that we have tried to be simple "catholic" (universal) Christians in a post-denominational era.

For whatever reason, the fact is that in the recent decades of the late twentieth and the early twenty-first century, Christian Churches and Churches of Christ have experienced significant growth.

The Rise Of The Megachurch

A part of this story is the growth of megachurches in our ranks. It is not, of course, as if there had never been large congregations among us. First Christian Church of Canton, Ohio, led by P.H. Welshimer and others, had been our largest congregation for decades, with the *Directory of the Ministry* reporting in 1964 over 6,900 members. (In the decades after the middle of the century the *Lookout* Magazine printed a weekly listing of our largest reporting Sunday Schools.)

But the national attention that came to be focused on conservative and Evangelical congregations like the Willow Creek Community Church in suburban Chicago foreshadowed the growth of large ("mega-") Christian Churches around the country. Think tanks like Fuller Seminary's Institute for Church Growth had for several decades encouraged congregations to plan, very intentionally, for such congregational evangelism.

The *Christian Standard* reflects this focus on such growth. In March of 1998 the *Standard* began a listing of our megachurches with an average weekly attendance for the year of one thousand or more. The listing of Sunday Schools was a thing of the past. In 2006 the criteria rose to a weekly average of 2,000 or more, and congregations between one and two thousand are listed as "emerging megachurches."

By February of 2008 Simon J. Dahlman's "Seen/Heard" column in the *Standard* reported (from the Hartford Institute for Religion Research) that of the nation's 1,331 megachurches (with an attendance of at least 2,000 persons), 38 were congregations of Christian Churches and Churches of Christ. Three of these exceeded an average attendance of 10,000: Southeast Christian Church

(KY), 18,013; Central Christian Church (NV), 12,000; and Christ's Church of the Valley (AZ), 11,500. Within the Stone-Campbell Movement, another fourteen of the nation's megachurches are identified with the Churches of Christ and one with the Christian Church (Disciples of Christ).

These megachurches, then, are part of the story of growth experienced by Christian Churches and Churches of Christ in the Nineties, and since the turn of the twenty-first century this growth appears to be continuing.

Identity (Crisis?)

As early as the 1980s some folk in Christian Churches and Churches of Christ began to sense some discomfort about our group identity and our relationship to the wider church. At one of the "Open Forum" meetings (Chapter 11) Robert Oldham Fife cited this apparent "crisis" in an unpublished paper entitled "What Do We Mean by 'Restoration' and of What?" He asked "Is the historic concern of this heritage—the plea for recovery of Christian unity through 'restoration,' for the sake of the mission to which Christ has called His Church—is that historic concern yet valid?"

There are probably a variety of reasons for this unease about identity. It was never our purpose to be particular or peculiar. Instead, as noted earlier, we sought to be faithful to simple New Testament Christianity as catholic believers, seeking to be "Christians only, not the only Christians." At least, that was our slogan. Furthermore, we see ourselves as not beholden to a connectional denominational structure, headquarters, or hierarchy ("independent" now, several decades removed from its origins, carries that sort of connotation for many of us).

Robert Fife

Adding to this is an unease, or even embarrassment, about our yielding to the temptation to be sectarian, legalistic, and isolated from other Christians. If our identity is too narrowly identified with a few items of correct doctrine (about baptism, for example), especially if that identity appears to suggest that we are the only Christians (rather than Christians only), then our self-identity will come under scrutiny.

For these reasons, and perhaps more, we are also tempted to be non-historical. Earlier in this volume (Chapter 1) we asked "Do We Have a History?" If we are now embarrassed about having become too sectarian, we may assume that this legalism comes to us from our movement's founders. Does it come, in fact, from the Campbells or Barton Stone? If it does, why would we want to study that history or want anything to do with it? Students of Thomas Campbell's *Declaration and Address* know, of course, that our history is not narrow and legalistic at its roots. Barton W. Stone is, for many, an "icon of Christian unity." And the writings of Alexander Campbell, viewed over the decades of his writing, follow in the steps of his irenic father. The failure to study that history, however, may leave us uninformed, and this can affect our sense of identity.

An "identity crisis" is doubtless one of the sad results of forgetting our history. Where there is no sense of history, there are often no roots (or at least no deep roots). Those of us who teach in our movement's church-related colleges can affirm the truth that the history of the movement is hardly taught at all in many of our churches. Students will sometimes say that they've heard the name of Alexander Campbell, but rarely can they discuss what he actually taught.

Part of the identity question, or crisis, rises from the fact that Christian Churches and Churches of Christ stressed "restoration" so heavily in the mid-twentieth-century. When, in the late Eighties and early Nineties, we began to recover a greater interest in the unity plea of our movement, we found ourselves asking theoretical yet very practical questions: How and with what considerations do we relate to the wider church? How do we deal with the theological questions? What beliefs allow us to find "unity" with other Christians? With all other Christians or only some? What does unity mean?

The fact is, of course, that all Christians are informed by someone's or some group's beliefs, and their Christian identity is thus shaped (even when they are not aware of it) by those influences. Our identity crisis, then, also involves how Christian Churches and Churches of Christ are related to influences that play on us from outside the movement.

Just as the self-identity of the Christian Church (Disciples of Christ) is flavored by the denomination's participation in Mainline Protestant circles, it is probably fair to say that the identity of Christian Churches and Churches of Christ, in recent decades, is influenced by our understanding of and relationship to the "Evangelical" movement in the United States. Are we "Evangelicals?" Is that our "identity," and if so, does it influence us? Should it?

We all want to be "evangelical." The word is rooted in the bringing of good news to the whole world, specifically the good news of God's work in the person of Jesus the Christ. We are all called to this task. Christian Churches and Churches of Christ have taken the imperative of evangelism seriously, and our growth would seem to manifest this.

The problem lies in the fact that words often take on added connotations. What exactly does it mean to be an "Evangelical?" The capital letter on the word recognizes a nomenclature for a person or a recognized group among Christians. It would be hard to have never heard of "Evangelical Christians" as a designated theological, social, or political group in the United States in the last two decades. Print and broadcast news organizations have reminded us about "Evangelicals" at great length.

For some of us to call ourselves "Evangelicals" is simply to affirm two basic priority commitments: to the authority of the Bible, and to evangelism. These two commitments are shared by the people of our congregations and the people of the wider Evangelical community, and our fellowship within Evangelicalism allows us to avoid sectarianism or isolation. These two commitments are common features of theological conservatives. Indeed, many in Christian Churches and Churches of Christ who label themselves Evangelicals use the terms "conservative" and "Evangelical" interchangeably, loosely meaning the same thing. All of this led one noted scholar to encourage us to recognize ourselves as Evangelicals, to affirm that Christian Churches and Churches of Christ are indeed "...in the evangelical group photo."

For others among us who share these conservative biblical and evangelical commitments, the discomfort lies in whatever added connotations the capitalized word might suggest. While welcoming dialogue with the Evangelical movement (we are, after all, a movement committed to the unity of the Lord's church), there is a concern that "Evangelicalism" rises from a history of Protestant beliefs and practices that the Stone-Campbell Movement does not historically share. Thus, identifying ourselves too strongly or exclusively with Evangelicalism could easily compromise core convictions (regarding the ordinances of baptism and the Lord's Supper, conversion, the nature of the church, and its relation to the state). Desiring as well to dialogue not only with Evangelicals but also with other Christian traditions, some among us prefer to see ourselves as a movement within the church and a group photo that uses a more "wide-angle lens."

All across Christian Churches and Churches of Christ there is a wide appreciation of some of the contributions of the Evangelical movement. The discussion centers around how we understand our own identity in relation to it. And, most importantly, how we understand our Stone-Campbell identity in relation to the whole church of Jesus Christ.

Identity, then, can be, and is, a sobering concern. It is certainly a live issue among us and probably will continue to be in the years ahead.

Concern for the Unity of the Movement and the Church

A relatively stronger focus among Christian Churches and Churches of Christ in recent decades is unity. It had never been absent, of course, but the weight of emphasis on restoration, seen in our self-denominated title of the "Restoration Movement," had impressed itself on our churches. This emphasis gave weight to apostolic teaching about baptism, the Lord's Supper, and the biblical writings that inform our views about these things.

But the cause of unity was always there. The Claude Witty/James DeForest Murch efforts of the 1930s and Murch's editorship of a journal for the blossoming Evangelical movement in the late Forties and early Fifties foreshadowed efforts to reach across lines between parts of the Stone-Campbell Movement and parts of the larger church.

As with Claude Witty, efforts to maintain dialogue within the segments of the Stone-Campbell Movement never lacked for champions. A series of Internal Unity Consultations between "Cooperative" and "Independent" Christian Churches was held in the late Fifties to mid-Sixties, but the weight of leadership came largely from moderates among the Independents, and the consultations died for want of interest and achievement. Among leaders of higher education, Dean E. Walker, President of Milligan College and then Emmanuel School of Religion, also tried to keep avenues of dialogue open with Cooperative Disciples, though with limited success.

From within Churches of Christ came two early heroes. Carl Ketcherside, editor of the Mission Messenger for many decades, experienced a dramatic change from his early "Sommerite" understandings and, from the mid-1950s onward, worked for peace and unity within the Stone-Campbell Movement. Ketcherside was a favorite speaker for college and career retreats for young adults from Christian Churches and Churches of Christ. Through the rest of his life (d. 1989) he preached the message that "Wherever God has a child, I have a brother or sister."

Leroy Garrett

Another editor and speaker from the Churches of Christ, Leroy Garrett, through his journal the *Restoration Review*, also championed the cause of unity. For the past half-century Garrett, a Harvard University

Ph.D., has encouraged a commitment to dialogue among the folk of the Stone-Campbell Movement.

Victor Knowles

From among Christian Churches and Churches of Christ came a similar spirit of desire to promote fellowship among the heirs of the movement. Victor Knowles, founder of Peace on Earth Ministries and editor of *One Body*, and Don DeWelt of College Press were early promoters of the Restoration Forum, an annual three-day gathering of fellowship for people from all three wings of the movement that met annually from 1984 through 2008.

Another effort for dialogue between the three major segments of the Stone-Campbell Movement began in 1999. Richard Hamm, General Minister and President of the Christian Church (Disciples of Christ), met with key preachers and educators from the Churches of Christ as well as Christian Churches and Churches of Christ. This annual meeting, known as the Stone-Campbell Dialogue, continues. Across the movement there is an acknowledgement of the sin of division in Christ's body and an affirmation of shared faith in Christ.

The emphasis on unity is also evidenced in the publication (2004) by scholars of all three segments, of *The Encyclopedia of* the *Stone-Campbell Movemen*t. Alongside the *Encyclopedia* are cooperative efforts of people from across the movement in the ministries of the Disciples of Christ Historical Society and the World Convention of Churches of Christ. The President for the 2008 World Convention, C. Robert Wetzel, is a leading educator from among Christian Churches and Churches of Christ.

We began Chapter 10 by noting the spirit of fellowship that was observed in 1909 at the Centennial Convention. Another century has now passed and Thomas Campbell's *Declaration and Address* is as relevant as ever. Rather than convening a bi-centennial convention in 2009 (the World Convention met in

Nashville in 2008), a committee of people from across the movement is encouraging a "Great Communion" to be held in local communities everywhere, bringing congregations from all three segments together to celebrate and give thanks around the Lord's Table. Remembering Thomas' two-hundred-year-old document will serve to remind us of our heritage of concern for the unity of Christ's people.

Questions for Discussion:

1. What additional factors may help to explain the growth of Christian Churches and Churches of Christ? Of those cited above, which ones do you think appear to offer some explanation for our recent growth?

2. What are the advantages of megachurches? Of smaller congregations? What are your experiences with various sizes of local congregations?

3. What do you make of this discussion of "identity" and "crisis?" Does a fellowship of churches like Christian Churches and Churches of Christ need "an identity?" If so, why, or why not?

4. When the T.V. news programs begin to cite "the Evangelicals" (capital "E"), do you think the newsreader is clear (in his or her own head) about the term? Are we, as Christians, clear about what we mean? Do you feel included? Do we need to be clear about these terms?

5. Do you sense that a greater concern for Christian unity has come to the fore in recent years among Christian Churches and Churches of Christ? How has that concern touched your own local congregation?

For Further Reading:

Baker, William R., Editor. *Evangelicalism and the Stone-Campbell Movement, Vol. 1*. Downers Grove, IL: InterVarsity Press, 2002.

Baker, William R., Editor. *Evangelicalism and the Stone-Campbell Movement, Vol. 2.* Abilene, TX: ACU Press, 2005.

Carson, Glenn Thomas, Douglas A. Foster, Clinton J. Holloway. *One Church: A Bicentennial Celebration of Thomas Campbell's Declaration and Address*. Abilene, TX: Leafwood Publishers, 2008.

Garrett, Leroy. *The Stone-Campbell Movement*. Joplin, MO: College Press, 1994. See pages 487-92, 525-40

Webb, Henry E. *In Search of Christian Unity: A History of the Restoration Movement*. 2nd Edition. Abilene, TX: ACU Press, 2003. See pages 421-35, 465-73.

Facing the Future as a Refugee Movement

What does the future hold for Christian Churches and Churches of Christ? The way we frame the question is important. "What does the future hold?" sounds as if we are in the hands of an uncontrollable fate. Perhaps we should ask, "What direction should Christian Churches and Churches of Christ follow in the future?" But that question places too much faith in our human ability to discern the right path. "What does God want us to be?" That's the proper question. We know he holds the future. What we hope and pray for is discernment to see his hand at work and a willingness to submit to his will.

The authors do not claim to be prophets who know that future. However, we do pray for discernment and wisdom, and offer the following thoughts.

Avoiding Amnesia

Facing the future, this small volume wants to suggest, depends on knowing what the past has taught us. Facing our future while in a state of amnesia will not work well.

Amnesia is a loss of memory. A loss of personal memory inhibits our answering questions like "What is your name?" or "Where do you live?" For Christians it limits, and certainly damages, our ability to answer questions like "What do you believe?" If we have convictions about unity, restoration, or mission, we owe a debt of gratitude to Stone, the Campbells, and others who are foundational to what we do in the future.

Facing the future, then, must build on our memory of where we have come from. In light of the heritage we sketched in the first twelve chapters, we believe God is leading us to consider the following directions.

Restored and Ever Restoring

The original dream of our movement was to bring unity to Christians by restoring to the church certain commitments and practices it had lost. Again, the metaphor of restoring a house comes into play. Parts of the house may be original and sound. Later additions need to be removed. Perhaps entire rooms have disappeared and must be rebuilt. So also with the church. We desired to restore the church that was in the mind of Christ and the Apostles.

Have Christian Churches/Churches of Christ restored that church? The answer must be "Yes and No." On the one hand, we have done great service to the church by restoring practices that were neglected in the religious setting of Stone and the Campbells. Our emphases on believer's immersion, weekly communion, and local church responsibility and leadership are healthy witnesses to other Christian groups. We should not abandon these contributions at the very time when many others are adopting them in a spirit of unity.

But in many areas, we must admit that we have not fully realized the mind of Christ and his Apostles nor restored some of the practices of early Christians. We do not have enough of the depth of spirituality and the prayer life that early Christians experienced. We do not challenge the dominant culture the way they did, sometimes at the cost of their property and lives. We do not have the expectation of the Second Coming of Christ that pervaded their lives. In these and many other areas, restoration is an unfinished work.

Is the whole idea of restoration unworkable? Are unity and restoration "oil and water," so to speak, divisive instead of unifying? Some think so. Perhaps they are reacting to the worst of our heritage, when some of us seemed to assume we had perfectly restored the church and were, therefore, the only true Christians.

Preserving and defending our restored house (church), it is difficult for us to find unity with those who have not done so.

It may be that too narrow a view of Scripture also contributed to a misunderstanding of restoration. We want to restore God's house according to the "pattern" of the Bible. But thoughtful hermeneutics remind us that the biblical picture of the church may not read like a blueprint. Instead, it is more like a heart-felt description of what God's house can be, a description from the Architect and Builder.

Sadly, there are those who, seeing that restoration is presented as a legalistic pattern or blueprint, reject restoration altogether. That rejection leaves an ecumenical notion of unity as the primary agenda of the movement. Thus, we have been too often tempted by the either/or options of being blueprint "restorationists" or abandoning the restoration idea entirely in favor of unity. This is an example of where our amnesia does not help us. Thomas Campbell's propositions in his *Declaration and Address* help us to avoid the oil-and-water conclusion about unity and restoration; he advocated both. The Apostle Paul, in 1 Corinthians (1:10-14), reminds us that good teaching (restoration) and unity are mutually necessary. To use a biological term, they are symbiotic. They live together, furnishing nourishment to each other.

Thus, the restoration goal can work as long as we see it as a journey instead of an achieved destination. This is more in line with the dream of Stone and the Campbells. We want to be a movement that serves the church by restoring. We hold firmly to our current biblical practices but we also seek to reclaim others we have neglected. We hold on to the best of our tradition but we move forward to what God calls us to be in a new generation. "Christian Churches and Churches of Christ" describes both what we are and what we strive to be: churches that fully embody the life and character of their Lord. We are not there yet, but we are on the journey.

This journey in Scripture is often described as a pilgrimage. Unfortunately, to call ourselves "pilgrims" still partakes too much of the American success story. The "Pilgrim Fathers" bring to mind Plymouth Rock, the first Thanksgiving, and the manifest destiny of European settlers, a far cry from the biblical picture of a pilgrim people. Perhaps a better term is "refugee." Refugees have no power and no home. They have fled one home and look for another, better one. They have not arrived but are on a journey.

We need to live as refugees. But why should refugees worry about restoring a house? Can refugees be restorers? Both "refugee" and "restorer" are metaphors for our relationship to God. Like all such illustrations, they have their limits, and may even seem at first to clash. We think both are helpful. We do want to restore certain biblical attitudes and practices to the church, but we must do so as those still on the journey of faith. That faith does not rest in our confidence that we have perfectly restored the New Testament church. It rests in a Savior who leads us on the way to the New Jerusalem, the true house of God where God will dwell there among us.

Our movement's churches are always at a crossroads. We can be a "church-among-the-churches" that is very much at home in our culture, enjoying its participation in the culture's prosperity and social success and believing that we alone are the fully restored church. Or we can be a movement of refugees, fleeing our success and materialism for refuge in the Prince of Peace. Refugees travel lightly and are willing to change. They are on the journey of restoration and unity, knowing that neither the church (the community of faith, the Body of Christ) nor our own movement (a community of concern within the church) will ever be completely what it should be, the former the spotless bride of Christ on that day when Christ presents the whole church to God, the latter a movement within the one church seeking to serve the whole Body.

Not the Only Christians

"We are Christians only, not the only Christians." The early leaders of our movement took the meaning of these words seriously. Thomas Campbell intended his *Declaration and Address* for "brethren of all denominations." Alexander Campbell preached in Baptist, Presbyterian, and other churches. In 1837 he said, "I observe, that if there be no Christians in the Protestant sects, there are certainly none among the Romanists…Therefore, for many centuries there has been no church of Christ, no Christians in the world…and the gates of hell have prevailed against his church!" Yet, there are some of us in Christian Churches and Churches of Christ who were raised to believe that we alone were Christians and that everyone in "the denominations" was lost.

This exclusiveness often reflected our claim that we are not a denomination. Are Christian Churches/Churches of Christ a denomination? Again, the clear answer is "Yes and No." Taken alone, denomination means "a named group." When *we* say "Christian Churches/Churches of Christ" *we* know who *we* mean. We know *our* colleges, *our* journals, *our* congregations. To a sociologist, we are a named group with a history and a group identity.

But part of the problem is that American culture interchangeably uses the words "denomination" and "church" to mean the same thing. To be in the United Methodist Church is to be in the United Methodist denomination.

It was never our intention to be either "The Church" (we're the only Christians) or "A Church." Barton Stone and his colleagues in the Springfield Presbytery decided that it was so much of a denomination that it should "die and sink into the body of Christ at large." Thomas Campbell's first proposition says it clearly: "The Church of Christ on earth is essentially, intentionally, and constitutionally one, consisting of all those in every place who profess faith in Christ, and [profess] obedience in all things according to scripture, and who manifest the same in their tempers and conduct…" The foundational principle of the movement was and is that there is only ONE church.

If being a denomination, therefore, means being "a church" or "the church" or "a church among the churches," then we do not aspire to be one. After all, our spiritual ancestors were not comfortable with either the language or the reality of denominationalism. Denominational boundaries fixed barriers to fellowship. Worse, they suggested that there was more than one church.

Are Christian Churches/Churches of Christ a denomination? Sociologically, as a named and identifiable group, Yes. In ecclesiastical terms (as "a church" or "the church"), No.

Then what are we? In the words of Robert Oldham Fife, "how may a people who exist as a distinct community within the Church, for the sake of witness unto the unity of the Church, avoid the negation of their witness by their very existence?"

Today we face at least three choices regarding our identity. We can insist that we are the only Christians and thus not a denomination. We are *The* Church. Or, secondly, we can acknowledge that we are a denomination alongside the others, a church among the churches, albeit enlightened on certain issues. Not the only Christians but "a church" of Christians in a particular way.

Or perhaps our identity lies in a third way. We now live in a culture that some call post-Christian or postmodern. It is a culture suspicious of institutions, including denominations. To many, name-brand religion means nothing. It is a post-denominational age. In this culture we have the opportunity to become more of what our early leaders envisioned: neither an exclusive sect nor a denomination, but a movement within the one church.

Fife answers his question above by advancing the idea that our identity lies in "the neglected alternative" of being "a movement." He defines a movement as "a community of understanding and concern which exists and serves within the Church, and for its edification." He argues that "a distinct people witnessing to the unity of the Church can only consistently be a movement within the Church."

"Movement," then, is far more than just a word to avoid being a "denomination." It is a self-understanding that allows us to teach and practice, with conviction, what we understand about baptism, or the Lord's Supper, or any other issue, without removing ourselves from the wider church. Movement language is, as well, pilgrimage language. It is refugee language. We can be people on the move, with conviction and unity at the same time. We could invite our fellow pilgrims with other names and understandings to journey with us. We can find common tasks of service in our communities with other pilgrims, we can share in worship at Thanksgiving, and dialogue with them as well, even when our scriptural understandings and convictions do not always match. We could be Christians only, not the only Christians.

A House of Prayer for the Nations

Such a movement would also serve the missionary church we want it to be. Unity and restoration, as far back as Campbell's *Declaration and Address*, were not the ends. They were means to the end that the world might believe (John 17:20-21). Missions and evangelism would not be merely a task for certain Christians, but would be at the heart of the movement and the whole church's identity. Evangelism is not recruiting people to our brand of Christianity but proclaiming the reign of God over all.

When Jesus threw the moneychangers from the temple, he said (quoting Isaiah), "My house will be called a house of prayer for all nations, but you have made it a den of robbers" (Mark 11:17). God intended his house, including Christian Churches and Churches of Christ, to be for all nations.

Our movement still has a long way to go in this regard. As noted earlier, we have too often followed and reflected our American culture regarding race relations. With few exceptions, we were not at the forefront of the Civil Rights Movement. Those of us who have attended the North American Christian Convention over the last half-century know that the crowds have been overwhelmingly white and middle-class. Our colleges have all too often reflected this as well. As one travels around the country, exceptions can indeed be found, but in general we are not out-in-front in regard to ethnic diversity.

We have also followed the culture concerning our view of men and women in our churches. Throughout this book you will find few names of women who were publicly notable in the movement. This is not because women were unimportant. Much of the important work in Christian Churches and Churches of Christ is, and has been, done by women: teaching, especially of children; reaching out to shut-ins; visiting the sick; comforting the grieving; and their contribution to our cross-cultural missions work has been of huge significance.

There have been, however, relatively few women with visible leadership roles (as presidents of conventions, colleges or seminaries, editors of our journals, executives of our mission agencies).

Clara Babcock

This is partly just a reflection of American culture at large, but therefore, at the same time, it calls for a recognition that we must be thoughtful about how we allow the culture to shape the church.

There are, to be sure, notable exceptions to the generalizations made in the previous paragraphs. In 1883 several missionary couples were ordained, setting aside these families for foreign missionary service. The ordinations of Clara Babcock (1888) and Sarah ("Sadie") McCoy Crank (1892) to preaching ministries in Christian Churches, and the fruitful results of their work, motivated an extended examination of the issue of women in the pulpit. The *Christian Standard*, from early in 1892 and well into 1893, opened its pages to a wide-ranging discussion of the topic. Whether in missions or in preaching, the role of women is not a new topic in our history.

We want to be biblical regarding the roles of men and women. Women should at least have the visibility they had in the New Testament, where they supported Jesus financially, worked as missionaries with Paul, and even had churches meeting in their homes. The early leaders of the Stone-Campbell Movement all supported the role of women "deaconesses" in the churches. Robert Milligan's *Scheme of Redemption*, in 1868, noted that "The diaconate of the primitive Church was not confined to male members... and it is to be regretted that it was ever discontinued in any Church."

Very few of our churches have elders who are women. The great influence of women in our churches is often manifested more indirectly. As a movement with no headquarters or hierarchy beyond the local church, there will be no single pattern for the ministries of men and women, and there will probably continue to be variations of practice from congregation to congregation.

While there are few overt racists or sexists today, it is fair to say that we have not resolved these issues. Christian Churches/Churches of Christ have the opportunity to restore the multiculturalism of the New Testament church. This will call on us for confession of sin where we have too easily reflected the prevailing culture, and for repentance that moves beyond symbolic acts to real change. In short, a refugee movement must welcome refugees.

Good News for Head and Heart

The future of Christian Churches/Churches of Christ must be more than an institutional pilgrimage; it must be a spiritual one. Our own critics have noted that we often focus on convincing the head while neglecting the heart. Leroy Garrett, an editor and observer among the Churches of Christ, acknowledges that there is some truth in this point, but he notes that it is "grossly overstated."

Alexander Campbell's series of articles "On the Restoration of the Ancient Order of Things" dreamed that the restoration of the weekly Lord's Supper, believer's immersion, and local church leadership would lead to a more spiritually disciplined church. It was not doctrine for doctrine's sake. We should "pray more and dispute less." The Supper was to be a spiritual feast, baptism a death to self and a rising to newness of life; therefore we need to be always reforming and deepening our understanding of these

Robert Richardson

ordinances, conducting them with care and devoting to them our time and attention.

A thinker who avoids amnesia, Garrett himself cites a litany of leaders in the history of the movement who have called us to the spiritual or devotional side such as Robert Richardson (mid-nineteenth century), the Campbells' biographer; the Campbells themselves in their family devotional life; Isaac Errett, the founding editor of the *Christian Standard*; Barton Stone as he shook hands with Raccoon John Smith; and the more recent Toyozo Nakarai, the internationally recognized biblical scholar and elder of his congregation. They remind us of "the spiritual side of our heritage."

Occasionally it is said that our movement is good in its theory, but that in its history the theory does not work. Dr. Garrett's words remind us that, whatever our movement's failings, the theory has in fact been admirably lived out in the lives of countless Christian folk. The reader can probably join Garrett in recalling such persons, men and women in our congregations who understand the movement's principles and who demonstrate them "in their tempers and conduct."

Lord, Come Quickly

The one certainty of the future of Christian Churches and Churches of Christ is that our Lord will come again. Without digressing to the theories of millennialism that have attracted the attention of some, it is important that, as a refugee movement, we live with a sense of anticipation. Jesus will return to take us to be with him forever.

The Second Coming relativizes all our plans and programs. God alone reigns, though we only see that reign by faith. Our journey is a servant of the ultimate destination: the heart of God. We must learn and remember to desire him alone.

As a part of the celebration of communion some congregations, after reading the words of institution, remind the church of these truths: "Christ has died; Christ has risen; Christ will come again." May he come quickly.

Questions for Discussion:

1. Is "restoration" still a workable concept and a noble goal? What do we mean by "restoration?"

2. What do we mean when we talk about Christian "unity?" How do we understand "unity?" And what are some

intentional, concrete ways we can work for unity in the church (the community of faith, the Body of Christ)?

3. If restoration and unity are means to an end, what do we understand that "mission" to be?

4. In what ways do you see Christian Churches and Churches of Christ ministering across the cultural lines that exist in our modern age?

5. What would you like Christian Churches and Churches of Christ to become in the next few decades?

6. Is it possible to have "pride" in our movement? If "yes and no," how so?

For Further Reading:

Fife, Robert Oldham. *Celebration of Heritage*. (Johnson City, TN: a compendium of the author's essays and articles, 1992). See pages 265-278 for "The Neglected Alternative," pages 443-462 for "The Stone-Campbell Movement: Toward a Responsible Future," and other related articles.

Garrett, Leroy. "The Spiritual Side of Our Heritage." *Christian Standard*. October 17, 1999. See pages 14-17.

Garrett, Leroy. *The Stone-Campbell Movement*. Joplin, MO: College Press, 1994. See pages 541-57.

Long, Loretta M. *The Life of Selina Campbell: A Fellow Soldier in the Cause of Restoration*. Tuscaloosa: University of Alabama Press, 2001.

Miller, Bonnie. *Messengers of the Risen Son in the Land of the Rising Sun: Single Women Missionaries in Japan*. Abilene, TX: Leafwood Publishers, 2008.

Nakarai, Toyozo W. *An Elder's Public Prayers.* Hicksville, N.Y.: Exposition, c1979.

North, James B. *Union in Truth: An Interpretive History of the Restoration Movement. Cincinnati*: Standard Publishing, 1994. See pages 353-69.

Pereira (Lantzer), Mary Ellen. *An Examination of the 1892-93 Christian Standard Controversy Concerning Women's Preaching*. Johnson City, TN: Emmanuel School of Religion (M.A.R. Thesis), 1990.

Richardson, Robert. *Communings in the Sanctuary*. Abilene, TX: Leafwood Publishers, 2000.

Study Guide

General Comments on Teaching *Renewal for Mission*

1 This study guide is written for small groups or church classes. It assumes that each student or family has a copy of the book *Renewal for Mission: A Concise History of Christian Churches and Churches of Christ,* and has read the appropriate chapter before the class meets.

2 Some Christians do not see a need for studying church history and may even see it as negative. There are many reasons for this. One is that Christian Churches and Churches of Christ have been deeply influenced by the American idea that the past is something from which we need to escape so we can move to a better future. Some resist the idea that Christian Churches and Churches of Christ have been shaped by the ideas and events of their past, seeing our origins only in scripture. The first part of chapter one responds to such objections.

3 Goals for the study of the history of Christian Churches and Churches of Christ in *Renewal for Mission* include:

a. to help members of Christian Churches and Churches of Christ understand more fully how they have been shaped by the people, ideas, and events of the past, especially the last two hundred years.

b. to explain and demonstrate the ideals that gave rise to Christian Churches and Churches of Christ in the nineteenth century and what we might draw from this heritage to strengthen our churches today.

c. to examine and evaluate the parts of our history that have been detrimental to our spiritual health so we might be humbled and strive for a more Christ-like existence.

4 The material in each chapter focuses on one main idea and has been kept to as manageable a level in both length and complexity as possible. Teachers may feel a need to do other background reading on each topic. The "For Further Reading" section at the end of each chapter lists materials that deal specifically with the subject matter for that chapter. If you want to add three or four key books to your library that will consistently be helpful in this study, the following are ideal:

a. Leroy Garrett, *The Stone-Campbell Movement* (College Press, 1994).

b. Henry Webb, *In Search of Christian Unity: A History of the Restoration Movement*, 2nd. edition (ACU Press, 2003).

c. Douglas A. Foster, et. al., *Encyclopedia of the Stone-Campbell Movement* (Eerdmans, 2005).

5 This study is not merely to learn historical facts, but to help shape us more into the likeness of Christ. Church historian Justo Gonzalez has said: "Every renewal of the church, every great age in its history, has been grounded on a renewed reading of history." Pray that this study will in fact be part of a process of spiritual formation that will renew and revitalize your congregation and Christ's church throughout the world.

CHAPTER ONE: Do We Have a History?

Teaching/ learning goals for this lesson include:

a. Point out and discuss ways the European background to the Stone-Campbell Movement helped shape it.

b. Develop an appreciation for the debt Christian Churches and Churches of Christ owe to those who came before us.

c. Identify strengths and weaknesses of the ideas and attitudes we have inherited.

Lesson Plan

1. Begin by reading 1 Cor. 10:1-12. Mention that Paul is giving the Corinthian church a history lesson. In verse 12 he indicates that knowing their spiritual history should make the Corinthian Christians humble. The same is true of us. If we take the attitude that we are standing (we have everything together and have no problems), we are in the very place where we are in danger of a fall. Follow comments with a prayer that asks God's blessing and guidance for this study to humble us and shape us more into Christ's likeness.
2. **Group Discussion:** Ask students in groups of two or three to talk about what they believe are the main ideas from the Protestant Reformation that have had a significant influence on what Christian Churches and Churches of Christ believe and practice today. Allow two minutes, than ask for three or four hands to quickly tell what they came up with. Note these on a whiteboard, overhead projector, or computer projector. Use these initial responses as a springboard for the first part of the class presentation and discussion.
3. Chapter One focuses on the Lutheran, Zwinglian, Anabaptist, and Anglican (English) branches of the Reformation. One **Lutheran** legacy was to reject the Roman Catholic system of "penance" that implied people could merit or earn their salvation. Another was the insistence that "Scripture Alone" was the source of what Christians believe and practice—not any creed, council, or Pope. **Group Discussion:** Why did the Lutherans emphasize these items? How have Christian Churches and Churches of Christ accepted these ideas or struggled with them?

4. One **Zwinglian** legacy not mentioned specifically in the book was the idea that only what is explicitly commanded by scripture can be practiced by the church—in other words, silence prohibits. In his churches, therefore, there was no music or singing in worship since he believed there was no scripture that authorized such in worship. **Group Discussion:** Is this idea a healthy one? How does such an attitude toward scripture impact how a congregation or movement carries out its mission in the world?
5. One **Anabaptist** legacy was strict separation of church and state. That was the immediate reason for rejecting infant baptism—only those who have accepted and been saved by Christ are proper subjects for baptism, not every one who is born into society. **Group Discussion:** How have traditional understandings of baptism in Christian Churches and Churches of Christ been like those of the Anabaptists? How different? Why?
6. One legacy of the **Anglican** Church was its claim to be a "Middle Way" [neither Catholic nor Protestant, but a New Testament Church]. Many in the Anglican Church, however, believed it had not been fully "purified" of what they saw as Catholic corruption. These Puritans included several groups. All the early founding leaders of Christian Churches and Churches of Christ came from one of those **Puritan** groups—the Presbyterians. That means at least two things: (a) they were Calvinists, and (b) they believed in church rule by "elders" (presbyters). **Group Discussion:** In what ways would you think the Presbyterian heritage of the early founding leaders of the Stone-Campbell Movement has shaped Christian Churches and Churches of Christ?
7. One important legacy from the **Enlightenment** is the emphasis that something had to be "reasonable," that is, compatible with human reason, to be true. John Locke emphasized the reasonableness of Christianity. He taught that true Christianity was based only on the clear unmistakable teachings of the New Testament. Locke assumed that all reasonable persons would be able to agree on what the "express" teachings of he Bible were. **Group Discussion:** What are the positive aspects of this idea? What potential danger can you see in such an assumption? Some potential problems include making human reason the one standard of truth, and the arrogance that accompanies the conclusion that one has arrived at all truth.

CHAPTER TWO: The Promise of Restoration in Early America

Teaching/ learning goals for this lesson include:

- **a**. Point out and discuss ways the American background to the Stone-Campbell Movement helped shape it.
- **b**. Develop an appreciation for the contributions of Smith, Jones, and O'Kelly to Christian Churches and Churches of Christ.

c. Identify strengths and weaknesses of the ideas and attitudes we have inherited.

Lesson Plan

1. "Begin by reading Galatians 5:13-18. Mention that the idea of freedom prevalent in America at the time of the Movement's beginnings was not the same as the biblical idea of freedom, which was freedom from selfishness to be able to serve others fully." Chapter Two focuses on the new religious situation that existed in America. All the religious bodies from Europe were transplanted to the "new world." Three important attitudes transformed these European influences: freedom, religious authority, and restoration. **Group Discussion:** What did "freedom" (or liberty) mean when it was applied to religion in America? What did religious people want to be free from?

2. One thing people wanted to be free from was the old religious authorities. Many didn't want anyone telling them what to believe or practice—they could read the Bible and understand it for themselves. **Group Discussion:** What are the positive aspects of this attitude? When accompanied by a strong individualism and confidence in human reason, what are the potential dangers in this attitude?

3. The idea of restoration implies that something has deteriorated or been altered to the point that it is not what it could be or ought to be. The Stone-Campbell Movement tended to emphasize the restoration of precise doctrines and practices of the early church. **Group Discussion:** What aspects of Christianity do you believe needed to be restored in the 1800s? What aspects need restoration today?

4. Two groups with roots in the American scene are the James O'Kelly Christians who broke with the Methodist Church, and the Elias Smith and Abner Jones Christians who broke with New England Baptists. **Group Discussion:** How do both of these groups reflect the three attitudes that characterized American Christianity? In what ways are these two groups different from one another? In what ways are these groups like Christian Churches and Churches of Christ in their beliefs, attitudes, and practices?

5. Close the class, if there is time, by asking each class member to jot down what he or she thought was the most important insight gained from the lesson. Ask for two or three hands of people who have not yet spoken aloud in class.

6. Close with prayer that God will use this study to shape us more into his likeness.

CHAPTER THREE: Barton Stone and Christian Unity

The teaching/ learning goals for this lesson include:

a. Describe the main events of the life of Barton W. Stone and his significance for the formation of the Stone-Campbell Movement.

b. Examine and analyze the events of the Cane Ridge meeting of August 1801 and how they affected the development of the movement.

c. Discuss the ideas of the Last "Will and Testament of the Springfield Presbytery" and how they have affected Christian Churches and Churches of Christ.

Lesson Plan

1. Begin by reading Ephesians 4:2-6 and 11-16. Follow the reading by a prayer that we might have a deep commitment to maintaining the unity of the Spirit in the bond of peace, as did Barton W. Stone.
2. **Group Discussion:** Ask for three or four hands of people who can tell one fact about the early life of Barton W. Stone.
3. **Group Discussion:** Why is it significant that Stone's religious training was at a Presbyterian school?
4. The Cane Ridge meeting was one of the most important events in what many historians call the "Second Great Awakening." Chapter three has a section describing the strange happenings at Cane Ridge and Stone's interpretation of them. **Group Discussion:** How do you understand what happened at the Cane Ridge meeting in August 1801? After three minutes, ask for three hands of persons who have not yet spoken to the whole class to report on what was said in their discussion.
5. Stone and the other Presbyterian ministers who helped with the Cane Ridge meeting got in trouble with the Synod of Kentucky (the Presbyterian body that was over them). The Synod of Kentucky was made up mostly of "Old Light" ministers who insisted on strict subscription to the Westminster Confession and denied that God used revivals to convert people. **Group Discussion:** Why would the members of the Synod of Kentucky be alarmed at what happened at Cane Ridge?
6. In 1803 Stone and four other ministers formed their own Presbyterian body—the Springfield Presbytery. Yet by June of the following year they dissolved that body and committed to be simply Christians, writing "The Last Will and Testament of the Springfield Presbytery," to explain their commitment. **Group Discussion:** Give the class four minutes to read the "Last Will and Testament" (it is contained in its entirety in the book). Ask them as they read to mark phrases that sound familiar to what they have heard before in Christian Churches and Churches of Christ. Also, ask them to mark any parts

of the document that have NOT been part of their experience in Christian Churches and Churches of Christ. Ask for four or five hands to tell one thing they marked that was familiar and one that was unfamiliar. Discuss these things.

7. Close with a prayer giving thanks for the godly example of Barton W. Stone who risked his livelihood and well being to work for the visible unity of Christ's church.

CHAPTER FOUR: The Coming of the Campbells

The teaching/ learning goals for this lesson include:

- **a.** Examine and evaluate the ideas of Thomas Campbell in his *Declaration and Address of the Christian Association of Washington.*
- **b.** Identify and analyze important life experiences of the Campbells that led them to begin their effort to reform the church.
- **c.** Discuss the relationship the Campbell churches had to the Baptist Associations.

Lesson Plan

1. Begin by reading John 13:34-35 and 15:5-8. Follow the reading by a prayer that we might have the desire truly to be disciples of Christ as did Thomas and Alexander Campbell.
2. The Campbells were from Northern Ireland. They lived in the midst of religious and political antagonism between Protestants and Catholics. They also, as members of the Church of Scotland, which was Presbyterian, were in the midst of religious controversy over a number of internal disputes. Each faction denounced the others, refusing to worship together or even recognize the others as Christians. **Group Discussion:** In groups of two or three, ask students to discuss for four minutes instances of religious conflict they have personally experienced or that they know about. After time is up, ask for three hands of people to briefly relate their experience. Then ask for three other hands to answer the question, what was really behind these instances of religious conflict?
3. Thomas Campbell came to America in 1807 and was assigned to preach in western Pennsylvania near Pittsburgh. When he served communion to Presbyterians not part of his faction, however, he got into trouble with the Synod which within two years expelled him. He formed, with the help of people who supported him in western Pennsylvania, an association to promote simple "evangelical" Christianity and the unity of the church. Campbell was commissioned to write a document to explain what they were up to. **Group Discussion:** Make a copy for every member of the class of Campbell's "Thirteen Propositions" that are part of the *Declaration and Address*. Hand these out and give the class members four minutes to read the

document individually. Ask them as they read to mark phrases that sound familiar to what they have heard before in Christian Churches and Churches of Christ. Also, ask them to mark any parts of the document that have NOT been part of their experience in Christian Churches and Churches of Christ. Ask for four or five hands to tell one thing they marked that was familiar and one that was unfamiliar. Discuss these things.

> Note: The thirteen propositions can be found at the end of the Study Guide. The full text of the *Declaration and Address* can be found at http://www.mun.ca/rels/restmov/texts/tcampbell/da/DA-CE.HTM

4. **Group Discussion:** Compare what you see in this small part of the *Declaration and Address* with what you saw last week in the "Last Will and Testament." What is the same? What is different?
5. Alexander, Thomas's oldest son, arrived in America with the rest of the family in 1809. Alexander married Margaret Brown in 1811, and when their first child was born, the issue of infant baptism arose. Based on his study, he decided that infant baptism was not valid and therefore he needed to be immersed as a believer. The only other group that practiced believers immersion was the Baptists. He persuaded a Baptist minister to immerse him along with his wife, parents, sister and two others. Not long afterward, the Redstone Baptist Association invited the Campbells' Brush Run Church to join the Association. They did so in 1815 and worked for reform as Baptist Churches for over fifteen years. **Class Discussion:** Ask the students in groups of two or three to discuss for three minutes what they think makes sense about the Campbell Churches being part of the Baptist Churches and whether or not they were surprised to find out about the Campbells affiliation with the Baptists. When time is up, ask for three hands to tell what they said.
6. Eventually, the Baptist Associations began to push the Campbell reform churches out. The Campbells themselves said they should never have separated from the Baptists. **Group Discussion:** Why would they say this, especially in light of the different understandings the groups came to have?
7. Close the class with a prayer of thanksgiving for the passion and courage of the Campbells to work for the unity and purity of Christ's church, and that we might also have that passion and courage today.

CHAPTER FIVE: The Stone and Campbell Movements Unite

The teaching/ learning goals for this lesson include:

- **a.** Compare and contrast the ideas and beliefs of Barton W. Stone and Alexander Campbell and their movements.
- **b.** Describe how many of the churches of the two movements united, creating one of the largest religious reform movements in America.
- **c.** Discuss how they were able to unite despite significant differences and what implications there are in this event for churches today.

Lesson Plan

1. Begin by reading Colossians 3:12-15. Follow the reading by a prayer that Christians would bear with one another in love as the members of the Stone and Campbell movements did when they united with each other to glorify God and strengthen His kingdom.
2. **Group Discussion:** The teacher should write out the seven classical categories of doctrine: God, Christ, Holy Spirit, Humanity, Salvation, Church, and Last Things/ End of Time. Then ask class members as individuals to write as many doctrinal differences in these categories between Barton W. Stone and Alexander Campbell that they can think of in the next three or four minutes. Tell them they can consult their books. After doing this as individuals, have them read their lists to one another in groups of two or three. Finally, call the whole class back together. Write all the differences the class members identified. Try to do it by writing the differences in the doctrinal categories.
3. **Group Discussion:** Again in groups of two and three, ask the groups to decide which of the differences was the most serious, and why.
4. The most famous early union of churches took place in late December 1831 and early January 1832 in Lexington, Kentucky. Read part of the account of the union, especially parts of the speech of Raccoon John Smith and the acceptance by Stone of the proposal for unity. **Group Discussion:** What allowed the two churches in Lexington to come together in December, 1831? Why didn't their differences prevent this from happening?

   One major point to be made in this discussion is that the union was not easy. It never is. Yet these people were so committed to making visible the truth that there is one body, they could not drop the quest when the difficult issues arose.
5. **Group Discussion:** Is the unity of Christ's church worth giving one's life to? What precisely might that commitment look like in Christian Churches and Churches of Christ today? In your congregation today?

6. Close the class with a prayer of thanksgiving for the example of those in our heritage who were committed to the visible unity of Christ's church, and asking for wisdom and discernment for how we can reflect that truth that there is one body in our circumstances today.

CHAPTER SIX: Growth of the Stone-Campbell Movement

Teaching/ learning goals for this lesson include:

- **a**. Name and analyze the things that contributed to the growth of the Stone-Campbell Movement before the Civil War.
- **b**. Evaluate the method of evangelism developed by Walter Scott which was extremely successful on the American frontier.
- **c**. Discuss how the things that made the Movement grow in the nineteenth century work today in Christian Churches and Churches of Christ for growth or decline.

Lesson Plan

1. Begin by reading Acts 2:36-39. Follow the reading by a prayer that Christian Churches and Churches of Christ as a whole and each of us as believers will be renewed in our zeal to take the good news of Christ to people around the world **and** into our own circle of contacts.
2. Walter Scott began preaching what he called the *gospel restored* that could be made memorable by using five fingers to make his points (he started with six points—but five worked better): faith, repentance, baptism, forgiveness of sins, gift of the Holy Spirit. **Class Discussion:** In what ways might Scott's five-finger exercise have been a welcome message to the people of the frontier? In what ways might it have become a legalistic system of checking off things to do? Contrast Scott's list with the list used by Christian Churches and Churches of Christ in the twentieth century: hear, believe, repent, confess, be baptized.
3. Literally hundreds of schools were formed by members of the Stone-Campbell Movement in the nineteenth and twentieth centuries. Almost all were liberal arts colleges—not schools to train professional ministers. The idea was that every Christian is a minister; therefore all students, regardless of major or chosen profession, should have a thorough education in scripture. This is the educational heritage of Christian Churches and Churches of Christ and is reflected in our schools and colleges. **Class Discussion:** Do you agree with Campbell's ideas about ministerial training? Why or why not? For those who attended a Christian University, what was your experience with Bible classes? Did they serve to create a certain kind of cohesion or uniformity among

Christian Churches and Churches of Christ? Do the colleges and universities serve a unifying function today?

4. For most of our history the religious papers served one of the most important roles in giving Christian Churches and Churches of Christ a sense of connectedness. The statement "Disciples don't have Bishops, they have editors" reflects a truth about who wielded power in Christian Churches and Churches of Christ. For Campbell, his papers and books (including the printed transcripts of his debates) served to get his ideas out to the widest possible audience. The most important of the papers of the day are mentioned in chapter Six. **Class Discussion:** Read the names of the papers there and see how many in the class have heard of them. If anyone knows something about the paper, let them tell it briefly.

   Again in groups of two or three, ask the class members to name the church paper they think is most influential in Christian Churches and Churches of Christ today. Give them one minute. This exercise may reveal that many of the class members know of NO church papers at all. Discuss the importance of the papers in the nineteenth century, then ask the following question. Do church papers (or other religious publications) have any impact on the broad membership of Christian Churches and Churches of Christ today? If so, how would you describe it? If not, why not?

5. The creation of the American Christian Missionary Society in 1849 was a milestone in the history of the Stone-Campbell Movement—some would say for good, and others for bad. **Class Discussion:** Why did those who organized the American Christian Missionary Society believe it was something needed? What objections might have been raised against the society? What is the significance of the society as far as what it says about the Movement?

6. Close the class with a prayer that God will again give this Movement a zeal for evangelism and the growth of Christ's church and kingdom.

CHAPTER SEVEN: Developing a Theology

Teaching/ learning goals for this lesson include:

- **a**. define theology and understand that all Christians "do theology."
- **b**. identify some main areas of theological discussion and development in the churches of the Stone-Campbell Movement.
- **c**. discuss areas of theology that are major topics in Christian Churches and Churches of Christ today

Lesson Plan

1. Begin by reading 1 Peter 3:15-16. Follow the reading by a prayer that we will be willing to do the sometimes hard work of study so that we can explain what we believe and why we believe it; but as importantly, that we can show in our lives what difference it makes to believe those things.
2. **Group Discussion.** In groups of two or three, ask students to discuss the concept of the term "theology" they have held during most of their life. Ask them not only to define it, but to explain how they have heard the term used (or not used) in church. Allow four minutes for this. Then ask for three hands to give a quick response each. After the three have spoken, ask for a show of hands as to how many had a **negative** feeling about the term and idea; ask one or two who don't usually volunteer to say why they had a negative feeling about the word. Then ask for a show of hands as to how many had a positive feeling. Again ask one or two to explain their feelings.
3. Theology is simply "thinking about God" or "thinking about faith." All Christians do it by necessity. We can do it well, or we can do it carelessly and not very well. **Group Discussion:** Ask class members to brainstorm on paper individually for about 90 seconds on the theological topics they have heard most emphasized in Christian Churches and Churches of Christ. Then ask class members to call out answers as you write them on the board. See what patterns emerge—do you see a focus on the Church? Baptism? The Bible? Lord's Supper? Historically these are some of the most prominent theological matters in Christian Churches and Churches of Christ since we saw ourselves as contending for something different from other religious bodies.
4. **Group Discussion:** Ask the class in groups of two or three to list all the different understandings of baptism that the different churches held in Campbell's time (as well as today). Give them three minutes. Then ask one spokesperson each from four groups (someone in each who had not spoken in the whole class yet) to tell one thing that other groups taught about baptism that was different from what the Stone-Campbell Movement taught.
5. **Group Discussion:** Discuss Campbell's views on the possibility of unimmersed persons being saved. What do you think his point really was? Why did he say the things he did when he was a very strong proponent of believers immersion—even to the point of refusing anyone who was not immersed membership in the churches of his reform movement?
6. Part of the point of the lesson is that we ought all be serious about theology, and that the Stone-Campbell Movement developed its own distinctive theology early in its existence. **Group Discussion:** Close

the class, if there is time, with a discussion of what theological matters the churches are struggling with today. Is such struggling a good thing or a bad thing?

7. End with a prayer for wisdom and discernment in our study and formulation of our beliefs and practices.

CHAPTER EIGHT: The Great Divide of the Civil War

Teaching/ learning goals for this lesson include:

a. examine ways the sectionalism of the Civil War and the accompanying racial attitudes shaped Christian Churches and Churches of Christ.

b. explain the role of the Civil War and sectionalism in the divisive issues of missionary societies and instrumental music in worship.

c. discuss the relation of the Christian to politics and war.

Lesson Plan

1. Begin by reading from Jesus' prayer for his followers in John 17:15-16. Follow the reading by a prayer that we will increasingly understand what it means not to be "of the world" as we reflect Christ's mission and not the world's values and actions.

2. Do a mini-lecture on the section of *Renewal for Mission* titled "Slavery and the Churches." **Group Discussion:** Ask the class in groups of two or three to discuss why the churches and leaders of the Stone-Campbell Movement took the positions they did regarding slavery. Give them four minutes. Than ask for three hands of people who will briefly report on the main idea discussed in their group.

   The point of this exercise is to reveal how powerfully the surrounding culture affects the thought and actions of the church. Slavery was an accepted way of life for many Americans; some today may even be able to argue like James Shannon that scripture does not condemn slavery, it only seeks to regulate slavery for the "benefit" of the black race (usually seen as inherently inferior). This reflects a certain view of the nature of scripture. If one sees the Bible primarily as a book of facts, one can certainly defend slavery with scripture. If one sees scripture primarily as the living, active word of God, the sword of the Spirit, which takes hold of our hearts and minds and shapes us into the likeness of Christ, then the practice of the owning of human beings will be seen for the inherently immoral practice it is and rejected by the church and Christians. The gospel is about transforming people into the likeness and mind of Christ.

3. **Group Discussion:** Discuss how the American Christian Missionary Society served as a divisive institution in the Stone-Campbell Movement because of the events of the Civil War. While there were some who objected to the missionary society for various reasons, it did not become an issue that divided churches until after the Civil War. Point out that even some of the society's staunchest opponents like Tolbert Fanning had refused to allow it to become a point of division until the Civil War events. What are the implications of these facts?
4. **Group Discussion:** Based on the previous discussions, have the class in groups of two or three talk about the sectional character Christian Churches and Churches of Christ for much of the twentieth century. Is it still true today? How do those sectional characteristics remain influential? How does racism fit into the picture?
5. **Group Discussion:** Discuss how doctrinal issues are never merely doctrinal issues. As we understand better the ways we have been profoundly shaped by cultural issues, we are equipped to see where that has sometimes been a detriment to our fulfilling God's intent for his church.
6. Close with a prayer that even as we throw ourselves into our culture to win people for Christ, that we will be able to discern and reject the "spirit of this world" wherever it is manifested in human culture, and that we will be formed more into the likeness of Christ.

CHAPTER NINE: Issues and Editors

Teaching/ learning goals for this lesson include:

- **a**. describe some of the major issues that divided the Stone-Campbell Movement in the late nineteenth and early twentieth centuries.
- **b**. identify the complex nature of the divisive issues—that they were more than simply biblical/theological disputes.
- **c**. explain and evaluate the attitudes of division and unity embodied in Daniel Sommer and T. B. Larimore.

Lesson Plan

1. Begin by reading Galatians 5:7-9; 15-26. Follow the reading by a prayer that even as we are serious about "running a good race," we never forget that the proof of that is whether we are characterized by discord, dissensions and division; or love, joy and peace.
2. **Group Discussion.** In groups of two or three, ask students to discuss for four minutes what they know about the division that resulted in Churches of Christ and Christian Churches or Disciples. Some possible specific questions might include: Did they hear anything at all

about the division when they were growing up? Is it news to them that the two groups were once one? Have they even heard of Churches of Christ and Disciples of Christ? If so, what are their impressions of the other groups? After the four minutes, ask for hands of three people to give a brief report on what their group said. After these three have spoken, see if there are any others with different responses. Allow a couple of minutes for this.

3. Next, the focus moves to the two "presenting issues"—the most visible and hotly contested matters, though by no means the only ones. These are the missionary society and instrumental music in worship. **Group Discussion:** Ask students to call out the pros and cons for each of the two matters. How did their defenders defend them, and how did their detractors oppose them? Write answers on the whiteboard, overhead, or computer projector. *Renewal for Mission* focuses primarily on the objections to these issues, but there were supporters who argued they were expedient ways of doing what God had commanded the church to do—evangelize the world, and worship Him. Though a few proposed that the missionary society was a necessary step in the Movement's maturity, no one insisted that these things were "essential" for the church to be the church. Opponents often pointed that out—that the supporters of these practices could drop them for the sake of unity without giving up anything essential if they really wanted to. Supporters believed that the conservatives' attitude was binding where Scripture had not bound, and that these expedients should be tolerated if it meant bringing more people to Christ.

4. **Group Discussion:** Discuss how the spirit of division could be seen in both the pro-society and anti-society people/ the pro-instrument and anti-instrument people.

5. **Group Discussion:** Assign half the class to take the position of Daniel Sommer and half the position of T. B. Larimore. (Divide the class however you see fit. You might simply do it by rows, or left and right side of the room.) Then in groups of four or five, have class members discuss and write out the strongest defense of their assigned person they can give. If you had to defend Daniel Sommer to a hostile crowd, how would you do it? If you had to defend T. B. Larimore to a hostile crowd, how would you do it? Allow five or six minutes for the discussion and writing of the defense. Monitor the groups and call time when it appears most have finished their assignment. Then choose a spokesperson from each "side" to come up to the front to defend Sommer and Larimore. Finally, open up a full class discussion on what they see as fundamentally at stake in the late nineteenth century concerning the unity of the Movement and the understanding of what the church really is.

6. Close class with a prayer that the spirit of division be removed from our hearts.

CHAPTER TEN: 1909-1949: Growth and Yet Further Division

Teaching/Learning goals for this lesson include:

a. To explain how Christian Churches/Churches of Christ came to have a distinct identity within the Stone-Campbell Movement: the issues involved, as well as the institutions, papers, and schools that began to manifest that identity.

b. To examine how the Cooperative/Independent division in the Stone-Campbell Movement was a long-term process rather than a single event.

c. To begin considering the issues that have unified our movement and those that have led to separation.

Lesson Plan

1. Begin by reading Ephesians 4:1-7. Follow the reading with a prayer for greater understanding of this scripture: how it relates to the church universal; how it relates to our movement's history; and what it teaches us as we try to understand our identity within the church and within the Stone-Campbell Movement.
2. Group Discussion: Depending on the makeup of your class, ask if anyone present grew up among the congregations of our movement before 1950. If there are, ask them to describe briefly their memories of that era. What leaders do they recall, what papers did they read, and what colleges did they support? What do they recall thinking (or feeling) about the difficulties of that time? Limit the time given to this discussion.
3. For a fellowship of congregations that is not officially connectional or tied legally to a denominational headquarters, informal rather than formal structures bind us together. Christian Churches and Churches of Christ developed, nonetheless, a sense of group-ness around a convention, around colleges, around a paper, and around certain ideas. **Group Discussion:** How did (and do they now) provide a sense of group identity for our churches? Relate this to your own congregation's sense of belonging to this movement.
4. When we study an era like this one (the first half of the twentieth century), we find ourselves looking at it in the light of scripture (the Ephesians passage, for example) and in the light of the work of the movement's founders (Stone and the Campbells). **Group Discussion:** How do we assess this era in the light of our heritage? How may it give

us some measure of pride? Or otherwise? To the degree that this era saw a second "division" in the movement, what was the nature of that division? Was it a division in the church? A division in the movement? Is division ever good? Is it bad? How should we think about these things?

5. Close with a prayer of thanksgiving for those who have gone before us (in the time of the Apostles, in Thomas/Alexander/Barton, and in the first half of the twentieth century). Ask that we be given godly understandings of who we are, knowing that God can bless us even when, in the service of Christ, we are flawed and we err.

CHAPTER ELEVEN: 1950-1990: Idenity and Activity

Teaching/Learning goals for this lesson include:

- **a.** To describe how Christian Churches/Churches of Christ emerged with a distinct identity within the Stone-Campbell Movement and within the larger church; to understand the nature of our cooperative work (colleges, conventions, etc.).
- **b.** To assess the role of "Restoration" in our self-understanding.
- **c.** To evaluate the idea of whether or not Christian Churches/ Churches of Christ are reflective of modern American culture, and the degree to which this is good or bad.

Lesson Plan

1. Begin by reading Galatians 3:23-26. Follow the reading with a prayer for understanding what it means to be, not under a custodian, but under faith, and thus able to respect and affirm fellow believers with whom we are one in Christ Jesus.
2. This era (1950-90) saw our fellowship of churches energetically give rise to the work of missions, evangelism, education, campus ministries, and even conventions. Group Discussion: Number the class off into groups of three, and instruct each group to assess the impact of all of this work: which ones were the major factors in the development of our group identity; which ones were the most effective; which ones best manifest the character of our segment of the Stone-Campbell Movement? Then have one person from each group report on why they assessed things as they did, remembering that there is not necessarily a right or wrong view.
3. Several people are specifically named in this chapter as leaders. **Group Discussion:** ask if anyone in the class knew, or knows, any of these people. Ask them to briefly talk about that person's influence and work. The leader of the class may add to this discussion if he or she also

knows of these leaders. Then ask for the names of other significant leaders from that era (in our colleges, great preachers, or editors). Discuss why these persons were significant in the era of this chapter.

4. Despite the development of an emerging identity for Christian Churches/Churches of Christ in this era, we were hardly in a "lock-step" conformity. **Group Discussion:** (again, use small groups within the class to discuss how issues were handled): did our congregations have a consensus about whether people in "the denominations" were Christian? In other words, did we live up to the old slogan "Not the only Christians, but Christians only?" Were there other issues that spawned differences in our churches (the charismatic movement? biblical literalism or inerrancy?). How well were these issues handled? Have each group give a brief report to the class, and try to sum up how diversity is dealt with in our churches.
5. Close the class in prayer, asking for God's guidance 1) for the cooperative ventures of our movement's congregations, 2) for finding our identity in Christ, and in being Christ to those around us, that the mission of the Lord's church might be fruitful.

CHAPTER TWELVE: Growth and Identity Crisis

Teaching/Learning goals for this lesson include:

- **a.** To examine the reasons for the growth of Christian Churches/ Churches of Christ: the post-denominational phenomenon, the use of church-growth methodology, the goal of a simple universal church, or other factors not discussed in the chapter that have affected that growth.
- **b.** To identify and examine the self-identity of Christian Churches/ Churches of Christ (a "crisis?"), and therefore to consider our relationship to the wider church and to other movements within the church universal.
- **c.** To examine and appreciate the recent efforts made to restore greater dialogue and fellowship within the Stone-Campbell Movement.

Lesson Plan

1. Begin by reading 1 Peter 2:21-25. Follow the reading with a prayer that our identity as Christian Churches and Churches of Christ will be centered on being Christ to others—that is, being willing to give ourselves for the sake of others, and not merely on having the "right" structures or in saying the "right" things.

2. **Group Discussion:** In the absence of a headquarters, hierarchy, or other required national institutions or structures, what is it that holds Christian Churches and Churches of Christ together? What role do conventions, papers, and colleges play? What shared beliefs and convictions do our congregations hold? Consider these questions in groups of three and then have each group leader report to the class as a whole.
3. **Group Discussion:** Again, in groups of three, work on these questions about "identity:" Do Christian Churches/Churches of Christ have an identity "crisis?" With what terminologies do we tend to label people: conservative? liberal? Evangelical? Protestant? What terms do you hear tossed about as descriptions for a college, a seminary, a paper, or even a specific congregation? Are these terms helpful? Harmful? Or, potentially, both?
4. Christian Churches and Churches of Christ are an identifiable segment of the Stone-Campbell Movement. **Group Discussion:** Go around the room and ask each class member about his or her knowledge of, and then experiences with, the other two parts of the Movement. Then, when everyone has shared whatever knowledge and experience they have, discuss how well the history of our Movement has been taught in our congregations: both the origins of the Movement, and its divisions.
5. Close with a prayer that we grow in our discernment of the true nature of the Lord's church and toward a maturity in Christ that enables us to serve others.

CHAPTER THIRTEEN: Facing the Future as a Refugee Movement

Teaching/Learning goals for this lesson include:

- **a.** To further examine our understanding of "restoration" and the implications of the definition we use, to see the relationship of restoration to being "refugees."
- **b.** To consider how restoration works alongside our concern for the unity of the church (assuming that we are "Not the only Christians").
- **c.** To define our terminology: church, sect, denomination, movement; and then to incorporate those definitions into the way we articulate our understanding of Christian Churches and Churches of Christ.
- **d.** To face, as honestly and fairly as we can, culturally-related issues in the life of our movement, recognizing the need to use mind, feeling, and action.

Lesson Plan

A note to teachers and learners: This final chapter and lesson is an attempt to project into the future the material that has been covered in previous chapters. The task before all of us in the Stone-Campbell Movement, and for the churches that are the particular focus of this volume, is to ask of us what we understand about what God would have us be in the twenty-first century. We bring to this task a heritage that is rich and unique in a variety of ways. At the same time, it is not unique, at least to the extent that we have tried to be simply "Christians only;" one of our old slogans was, after all, "In faith, unity (*i.e.* faith in Christ), in opinions, liberty, and in all things, love." We bring to this discussion both positive and negative experiences. This is, therefore, a lesson that depends on where you and your congregational leaders see our movement going. The entire history of the movement—-and, for purposes of this volume, the last three chapters in a special way—-call for all of us to make our ideas and understandings come alive in the way we approach the future.

1. Begin by reading Ephesians 4:11-16. Follow the reading with a prayer that we will not be complacent in our Christian journey, thinking that we have arrived. Pray that we will earnestly desire the sort of maturity in Christ that signals our growing up in every way into him who is the head, into Christ.
2. **Group Discussion:** Ask first if there is anyone in the class who has not heard the nomenclature "Restoration Movement." For those who grew up around that name, ask them what they thought it meant when they were young. Was it thought of as something that we had already accomplished? If so, how so? Ask what they think of the idea that it is always out there as a goal, something to strive for. Then ask how this notion of restoration fits with the idea of being a refugee. Do we see "refugee" as a negative word? Has anyone in the class ever known a political refugee? Does it make anyone in the class nervous to think of Christians as refugees? Is there a better word?
3. Using a screen or board, make a list of possible shared ministries that your congregation might do with other churches in your town (a Thanksgiving worship service together? Interfaith Hospitality Network care of the homeless? Tutoring persons in the community working on a GED? After-school programs for the children of single parents? etc.). Then pose this **question for discussion:** how does recognizing and acting out the given unity of Christ's people, in such cooperative ventures, promote the restoration of the church that was in the mind of Christ and his Apostles?

4. We live in a culture that says that words are "just rhetoric," that it doesn't really make any difference what words we use. In this and previous chapters, the word "church" (singular) has been used for the ONE church (and "churches" for local assemblies that are the church in that particular location). **Group Discussion:** form groups of five or six persons to discuss the importance of terminology. Here are some questions that might be helpful. What do people think of when they hear the word "church?" What might Matt. 16:18 suggest to us? Are Christian Churches and Churches of Christ "The Christian Church?" Are Christian Churches/Churches of Christ collectively, "a church?" On a practical level, how does our definition of these terms sect, denomination, church, movement show up in the way we live our congregational life. Ask a reporter from each group to share with the whole class.
5. For a **Group Discussion** of the class as a whole, use these questions. Are we pulled in two directions at the same time in relating to our culture? 1) We need to be culturally relevant to our community in order to reach people for Christ, but at the same time 2) we are lulled, perhaps unintentionally, into reflecting that culture when there is a better Christian way? In what additional ways, other than race and gender, do we confront this dilemma?
6. If time permits, ask the class: is it appropriate to have pride in our movement? Those of us who do have such pride must, of course, define the term carefully and explain how we are able to express that pride. But it's an important question.
7. End the class and the series with a time of group prayer, designating the person who will bring it to a close. Allow people to give thanks for our heritage and for the whole Church of Jesus Christ, and for renewal and growth unto our maturity in Christ. Allow, even encourage at the outset, times of silence; silence is okay. And with the "Amen," sing the "Doxology" (or some other brief song that everyone knows).

Thirteen Propositions from the Declaration and Address of the Christian Association of Washington, PA

PROP. 1. That the Church of Christ upon earth is essentially, intentionally, and constitutionally one; consisting of all those in every place that profess their faith in Christ and obedience to him in all things according to the Scriptures, and that manifest the same by their tempers and conduct, and of none else; as none else can be truly and properly called Christians.

2. That although the Church of Christ upon earth must necessarily exist in particular and distinct societies, locally separate one from another, yet there ought to be no schisms, no uncharitable divisions among them. They ought to receive each other as Christ Jesus hath also received them, to the glory of God. And for this purpose they ought all to walk by the same rule, to mind and speak the same thing; and to be perfectly joined together in the same mind, and in the same judgment.

3. That in order to this, nothing ought to be inculcated upon Christians as articles of faith; nor required of them as terms of communion, but what is expressly taught and enjoined upon them in the word of God. Nor ought anything to be admitted, as of Divine obligation, in their Church constitution and managements, but what is expressly enjoined by the authority of our Lord Jesus Christ and his apostles upon the New Testament Church; either in express terms or by approved precedent.

4. That although the Scriptures of the Old and New Testaments are inseparably connected, making together but one perfect and entire revelation of the Divine will, for the edification and salvation of the Church, and therefore in that respect can not be separated; yet as to what directly and properly belongs to their immediate object, the New Testament is as perfect a constitution for the worship, discipline, and government of the New Testament Church, and as perfect a rule for the particular duties of its members, as the Old Testament was for the worship, discipline, and government of the Old Testament Church, and the particular duties of its members.

5. That with respect to the commands and ordinances of our Lord Jesus Christ, where the Scriptures are silent as to the express time or manner of performance, if any such there be, no human authority has power to interfere, in order to supply the supposed deficiency by making laws for the Church; nor can anything more be required of Christians in such cases, but only that they so observe these commands and ordinances as will evidently answer the declared and obvious end of their institution. Much less has any human authority power to impose new commands or ordinances upon the Church, which our Lord Jesus Christ has not enjoined. Nothing ought to be received into the faith or worship of the Church, or be made a term of communion among Christians, that is not as old as the New Testament.

6. That although inferences and deductions from Scripture premises, when fairly inferred, may be truly called the doctrine of God's holy word, yet are they not formally binding upon the consciences of Christians farther than they perceive the connection, and evidently see that they are so; for their faith must not stand in the wisdom of men, but in the power and veracity of God. Therefore, no such deductions can be made terms of communion, but do properly belong to the after and progressive edification of the Church. Hence, it is evident that no such deductions or inferential truths ought to have any place in the Church's confession.

7. That although doctrinal exhibitions of the great system of Divine truths, and defensive testimonies in opposition to prevailing errors, be highly expedient, and the more full and explicit they be for those purposes, the better; yet, as these must be in a great measure the effect of human reasoning, and of course must contain many inferential truths, they ought not to be made terms of Christian communion; unless we suppose, what is contrary to fact, that none have a right to the communion of the Church, but such as possess a very clear and decisive judgment, or are come to a very high degree of doctrinal information; whereas the Church from the beginning did, and ever will, consist of little children and young men, as well as fathers.

8. That as it is not necessary that persons should have a particular knowledge or distinct apprehension of all Divinely-revealed truths in order to entitle them to a place in the Church; neither should they, for this purpose, be required to make a profession more extensive than their knowledge; but that, on the contrary, their having a due measure of Scriptural self-knowledge respecting their lost and perishing condition by nature and practice, and of the way of salvation through Jesus Christ, accompanied with a profession of their faith in and obedience to him, in all things, according to his word, is all that is absolutely necessary to qualify them for admission into his Church.

9. That all that are enabled through grace to make such a profession, and to manifest the reality of it in their tempers and conduct, should consider each other as the precious saints of God, should love each other as brethren, children of the same family and Father, temples of the same Spirit, members of the same body, subjects of the same grace, objects of the same Divine love, bought with the same price, and joint-heirs of the same inheritance. Whom God hath thus joined together no man should dare to put asunder.

10. That division among the Christians is a horrid evil, fraught with many evils. It is antichristian, as it destroys the visible unity of the body of Christ; as if he were divided against himself, excluding and excommunicating a part of himself. It is antiscriptural, as being strictly prohibited by his sovereign authority; a direct violation of his express command. It is antinatural, as it excites Christians to contemn, to hate, and oppose one another, who are bound by the highest and most endearing obligations to love each other as brethren, even as Christ has loved them. In a word, it is productive of confusion and of every evil work.

11. That (in some instances) a partial neglect of the expressly revealed will of God, and (in others) an assumed authority for making the approbation of human opinions and human inventions a term of communion, by introducing them into the constitution, faith, or worship of the Church, are, and have been, the immediate, obvious, and universally-acknowledged causes, of all the corruptions and divisions that ever have taken place in the Church of God.

12. That all that is necessary to the highest state of perfection and purity of the Church upon earth is, first, that none be received as members but such as having that due measure of Scriptural self-knowledge described above, do profess their faith in Christ and obedience to him in all things according to the Scriptures; nor, secondly, that any be retained in her communion longer than they continue to manifest the reality of their profession by their temper and conduct. Thirdly, that her ministers, duly and Scripturally qualified, inculcate none other things than those very articles of faith and holiness expressly revealed and enjoined in the word of God. Lastly, that in all their administrations they keep close by the observance of all Divine ordinances, after the example of the primitive Church, exhibited in the New Testament; without any additions whatsoever of human opinions or inventions of men.

13. Lastly. That if any circumstantials indispensably necessary to the observance of Divine ordinances be not found upon the page of express revelation, such, and such only, as are absolutely necessary for this purpose should be adopted under the title of human expedients, without any pretense to a more sacred origin, so that any subsequent alteration or difference in the observance of these things might produce no contention nor division in the Church.